Summary

Emerging from the Shadows

Steps to Recognize, Understand, and Heal from Gaslighting: A Comprehensive Recovery Workbook

Vivienne Holt

Chapter 1: Introduction to Gaslighting Dynamics

Gaslighting is a psychological manipulation technique that seeks to undermine a person's perception of reality. It involves the intentional distortion of information, leading the victim to doubt their own thoughts, feelings, and experiences. Gaslighting can occur in various settings, such as relationships, workplaces, or even within families. In this chapter, we will explore the intricacies of gaslighting dynamics, its origins, and its impact on victims.

The Origins of Gaslighting

The term "gaslighting" originates from a 1938 play titled "Gas Light," written by Patrick Hamilton. The play was later adapted into two films, with the most famous being the 1944 version starring Ingrid Bergman and Charles Boyer. In the story, a manipulative husband deliberately deceives his wife, making her question her own sanity.

While the term might be relatively new, gaslighting has been present throughout history in various forms. Its roots lie in power imbalances and the desire to control and dominate others. By distorting reality, the gaslighter gains power over their victim, eroding their self-worth and confidence.

Identifying Gaslighting Dynamics

Gaslighting can manifest in subtle and overt ways, making it difficult for victims to recognize and break free from its grip. The following signs may indicate the presence of gaslighting dynamics:

1. Denial and Invalidating: Gaslighters often dismiss or invalidate a victim's thoughts, feelings, or experiences. They might say things such as, "You're overreacting" or "That never happened." By belittling the victim's reality, the gaslighter undermines their confidence and self-trust.

2. Blaming and Shaming: Gaslighters tend to shift blame onto their victims, making them feel responsible for the issues at hand. They may use tactics like guilt-tripping, accusing, or shaming the victim to manipulate and control them further.

3. Confusion and Contradiction: Gaslighters often present contradicting information or manipulate the narrative to confuse their victims. By constantly changing the facts, they instill doubt and make it difficult for the victim to maintain a consistent perspective.

4. Isolation: Gaslighters often isolate their victims from family, friends, or support networks. By cutting off these connections, they gain more control over the victim's reality, as they become the sole source of influence in their lives.

5. Gaslighting by Proxy: Sometimes, gaslighters recruit others to

reinforce their manipulation. Friends, family members, or colleagues may unknowingly become enablers, further isolating the victim and validating the gaslighter's tactics.

6. Withholding Information: Gaslighters may intentionally withhold information, creating a power imbalance in the dynamics. By controlling access to knowledge, they can distort the victim's understanding of events and maintain their position of authority.

The Impact of Gaslighting

Gaslighting can have severe and long-lasting effects on victims' mental and emotional well-being. Some common consequences include:

1. Erosion of Self-Confidence: By constantly doubting their own perceptions, victims' confidence diminishes over time. They become reliant on the gaslighter's version of events and may struggle to make decisions or trust their instincts.

2. Emotional Instability: Gaslighting often leads to heightened anxiety, depression, and feelings of worthlessness. Victims may experience intense emotional swings, as the gaslighter's manipulation disrupts their sense of self and stability.

3. Cognitive Dissonance: Due to the conflicting information they receive, victims may experience cognitive dissonance – a state of mental discomfort caused by holding contradictory beliefs

simultaneously. This internal conflict can lead to confusion, frustration, and indecisiveness.

4. Obsession with Seeking Validation: Victims of gaslighting frequently seek external validation to validate their own experiences. They may constantly ask others for affirmation, struggling to trust their own judgment.

5. Dissociation: In severe cases, gaslighting can lead to dissociation, a defense mechanism where individuals detach from their thoughts, feelings, and memories as a way to protect themselves from further emotional harm.

Breaking Free from Gaslighting

Escaping the clutches of gaslighting is a challenging journey, but it is possible. Here are a few steps victims can take:

1. Educate Yourself: Understanding gaslighting dynamics is the first step towards breaking free. By identifying the signs and patterns of gaslighting, victims can gain clarity and develop a stronger sense of self-awareness.

2. Seek Support: Reach out to trusted friends, family, or professionals who can provide emotional support and guidance. Sharing your experiences with others can validate your reality and help you regain confidence.

3. Focus on Self-Care: Prioritize self-care activities that promote your mental, emotional, and physical well-being. Engaging in activities you enjoy, practicing mindfulness, and seeking therapy can aid in rebuilding your sense of self.

4. Set Boundaries: Establish clear boundaries to protect yourself from further manipulation. Communicate your needs and expectations assertively, refusing to accept any behavior that undermines your reality or self-worth.

Understanding gaslighting dynamics is crucial to recognize and counteract this destructive manipulation technique. By shedding light on its origins, signs, and impact, this chapter has provided a foundation for further exploration. Victims of gaslighting are not alone, and with the right knowledge, support, and resilience, they can break free from its grasp and regain their sense of self-worth and reality.

Understanding Gaslighting: Definition and Origins

Gaslighting is a term that has gained much attention in recent years, particularly within the fields of psychology and interpersonal relationships. It refers to a manipulative behavior pattern where one person covertly undermines another's perception of reality, leading them to question their own sanity, memories, or judgment. While gaslighting has become a popular buzzword, its origins and deeper understanding remain critical for recognizing and addressing this destructive form of psychological manipulation. In this chapter, we will delve into the definition, historical roots, and various manifestations of gaslighting, shedding light on this pervasive and harmful dynamic.

Defining Gaslighting:

Gaslighting, often described as a form of mental abuse, takes its name from a 1938 play titled "Gas Light" by Patrick Hamilton. The story revolves around a husband who systematically manipulates his wife into questioning her sanity by gradually dimming the gas lights and denying any changes are taking place. The term "gaslighting" has since evolved to encapsulate a broader range of manipulative tactics aimed at making someone doubt their perceptions, intuition, or memories.

At its core, gaslighting involves the gradual erosion of a person's self-confidence, self-esteem, and overall sense of reality. The gaslighter might employ subtle or overt techniques to distort facts, fabricate lies, or instigate confusion to gain power and control over their victim. Such manipulation can occur in personal relationships, workplace dynamics, and even within societal structures.

Historical Origins of Gaslighting:

While "Gas Light" is often associated with the origins of gaslighting, the behaviors it portrays predate the play itself. Throughout history, manipulative strategies akin to gaslighting have been employed by individuals seeking to exert control or maintain social hierarchy. However, societal, cultural, and gender dynamics have profoundly influenced the prevalence and patterns of gaslighting across different time periods.

Psychological Manipulation in Historical Contexts:

In the earlier centuries, rigid societal structures often paved the way for gaslighting dynamics. For example, during the Salem witch trials in the late 17th century, innocent individuals, mostly women, were subjected to gaslighting techniques, leading them to doubt their own innocence and admit to being witches. The tactics employed were similar to those seen in modern instances of gaslighting, including public shaming, isolation, intimidation, and distortion of evidence.

In the early stages of psychology as a formal discipline, gaslighting behaviors were also observed and studied. Sigmund Freud, the father of psychoanalysis, emphasized the significance of self-doubt and its origins in early childhood experiences. He discussed how parental figures can manipulate their children's perception of reality, leading to long-lasting effects on their psyches.

Gaslighting in Intimate Relationships:

Gaslighting is perhaps most commonly associated with romantic relationships due to its intimate nature and potential for long-lasting emotional harm. In these dynamics, gaslighting tactics can be subtle or blatant, designed to create dependency, undermine the victim's autonomy, and exert control.

For instance, the gaslighter may repeatedly deny events or conversations that happened, dismiss the victim's emotions, or manipulate situations and turn them around to make the victim feel guilty. Over time, these tactics can lead the victim to doubt their own sense of reality and rely excessively on the gaslighter's version of events.

Gaslighting in the Workplace:

Beyond intimate relationships, gaslighting can infiltrate professional settings, where power dynamics and hierarchies often amplify manipulative behaviors. Gaslighting may occur through constant invalidation of an employee's knowledge, skills, or past accomplishments, creating a toxic work environment that undermines their confidence and sense of competence.

Moreover, gaslighting in the workplace may take the form of manipulating the victim's perceptions of fairness, causing them to question their worth and accept unequal treatment. This can severely affect productivity, job satisfaction, and mental well-being.

Recognizing and Addressing Gaslighting:

Recognizing gaslighting requires awareness of the signs, which often include a persistent feeling of confusion, self-doubt, and a sense of being manipulated. Victims may also experience anxiety, depression, or a loss of self-esteem over time. Education and empathy play a vital role in addressing gaslighting, as victims need to feel heard and understood during their healing process.

It is crucial to create safe spaces for individuals experiencing gaslighting, whether through therapy, support groups, or conversations with trusted friends and family members.

Empowering individuals with knowledge about gaslighting techniques helps them regain confidence in their own perceptions and develop coping mechanisms to counteract manipulative behaviors.

Understanding gaslighting is essential for unveiling the often insidious methods used by manipulative individuals to undermine the reality and well-being of their victims. This chapter has explored the definition, historical origins, and various manifestations of gaslighting, emphasizing its presence in intimate relationships and the workplace. By shedding light on this destructive behavior, we can empower individuals to recognize, address, and heal from the emotional scars of gaslighting, fostering healthier and more empathetic relationships in all aspects of life.

Gaslighting's Shadows: The Impact on Personal Identity

Gaslighting is a psychological manipulation tactic that involves the manipulation and distortion of someone's reality. Its sinister nature lies in its ability to make individuals doubt their perception of reality, leading to a loss of personal identity. In this chapter, we will explore the insidious effects of gaslighting, discussing its origins, tactics employed, and the profound impact it has on shaping an individual's sense of self.

Origins of Gaslighting

The term "gaslighting" finds its roots in a 1938 play titled "Gaslight" by Patrick Hamilton. This play tells the story of a husband manipulating his wife into questioning her own sanity by subtly altering her environment. He would dim the gaslights in their home but then deny that anything had changed, making her doubt her own perceptions.

Gaslighting Tactics

Gaslighting can manifest in various ways, all aimed at undermining an individual's self-confidence and reality. These tactics may include:

1. Denial and Deception: Gaslighters frequently deny their actions or twist the truth, causing their victims to question their own memory

or experiences. By continually denying legitimate occurrences, they create doubt in the victim's mind.

2. Withholding Information: Gaslighters selectively withhold information, leaving their victims in a state of confusion. This intentional vagueness further erodes trust and distorts reality, making it easier for the gaslighter to manipulate the narrative.

3. Diminishing Feelings and Experiences: Gaslighters often invalidate their victim's emotions, making them feel as though their feelings are unjustified or exaggerated. They may dismiss their concerns or belittle their experiences, leaving the victim feeling unsure and uncertain.

4. Blaming the Victim: Gaslighters expertly shift blame onto their victims, making them question their own role in the manipulative dynamic. This tactic leaves individuals feeling responsible for the gaslighting behavior or believing they deserve the mistreatment they are enduring.

Impact on Personal Identity

Gaslighting can have significant and lasting effects on an individual's personal identity. The manipulation of one's perception and reality leads to a deep erosion of self-confidence, autonomy, and self-esteem. The following sections delve into the specific ways gaslighting impacts personal identity:

1. Self-Doubt and Insecurity: Gaslighting leads individuals to question their own thoughts, feelings, and memories. Over time, this constant questioning erodes self-trust and fosters deep-rooted self-doubt. Victims find themselves perpetually second-guessing their judgment and decisions, leading to a loss of confidence in their own capabilities.

2. Loss of Autonomy: Gaslighters aim to establish control by diminishing their victims' ability to make decisions for themselves. By eradicating personal autonomy, individuals become dependent on the gaslighter's judgments, causing them to detach from their own desires and beliefs. This loss of agency further erodes personal identity.

3. Cognitive Dissonance: Gaslighting creates an internal conflict within victims, giving rise to cognitive dissonance. The dissonance arises from the disparity between their own experiences or perceptions and the alternative narrative imposed by the gaslighter. This internal conflict fragments a person's sense of self and creates confusion and emotional turmoil.

4. Identity Displacement: Gaslighting can manipulate an individual's sense of self to the point where they adopt the gaslighter's version of reality. Victims may start to believe they are the cause of their own suffering, internalizing the gaslighter's blame and losing their authentic identity in the process.

5. Emotional Exhaustion: Gaslighting is an emotionally draining

experience. The constant manipulation, deception, and psychological abuse take a toll on the victim's emotional well-being. This exhaustion can lead to a persistent sense of anxiety, depression, and emotional instability, further eroding one's personal identity.

Gaslighting's insidious impact on personal identity is undeniable. Its ability to manipulate an individual's perception of reality can lead to the erosion of self-confidence, autonomy, and self-esteem. It is crucial to recognize the signs of gaslighting and provide support to those who have fallen victim to this destructive form of manipulation.

By fostering awareness, we can help restore personal identity and empower individuals to reclaim their truth and regain their sense of self.

Society's Silent Accomplice: How Culture Amplifies Gaslighting

In the realm of psychological manipulation, gaslighting is a term that has gained significant recognition in recent years. Defined as a form of emotional abuse, gaslighting involves an individual systematically undermining another's perception of reality, ultimately leaving them doubting their own sanity and questioning their sense of self. While gaslighting can occur in various relationships, be it intimate partnerships or workplace dynamics, society as a whole plays a significant role in amplifying this insidious practice. This chapter aims to delve into the ways in which our culture inadvertently contributes to gaslighting, perpetuating a society that is complicit in its silent acceptance.

Understanding Gaslighting:

Before we explore the cultural dimensions of gaslighting, it is imperative to grasp the foundations of this deeply damaging behavior. Gaslighting is rooted in power dynamics, where the gaslighter seeks to establish dominance over their target by distorting their perception of reality. Tactics like denial, trivialization, manipulation, redirection, and isolation are commonly employed to achieve this objective. The consequences for the victim can be devastating, leading to a loss of confidence, emotional turmoil, and an erosion of personal boundaries.

Media and Gaslighting:

One prominent avenue through which society inadvertently amplifies gaslighting is the media. Popular media platforms, such as television, movies, and social media, often perpetuate harmful narratives that normalize gaslighting behaviors. In romantic comedies, for instance, we frequently witness characters manipulating their partners' emotions and experiences, making light of this harmful behavior under the guise of romantic pursuit. These depictions create a distorted perception of what constitutes a healthy relationship, which, in turn, allows gaslighting to slip into the fabric of our societal norms.

Furthermore, the rise of social media has provided gaslighters with an amplified platform. Online spaces offer an anonymous shield behind which individuals can manipulate others by spreading misinformation, targeting vulnerabilities, or fostering a toxic online environment. The viral spread of fake news, the dissemination of harmful rumors, and the relentless onslaught of cyberbullying are all demonstrations of how online spaces can serve as breeding grounds for gaslighting behavior.

Gender Roles and Gaslighting:

Gender dynamics within society also contribute to the amplification of gaslighting tactics. Historically, women have been disadvantaged in terms of societal power, and this power imbalance is frequently exploited through gaslighting. In a patriarchal culture, women are often subjected to gaslighting tactics that aim to undermine their experiences, perceptions, and emotions. This perpetuates a cycle where women begin to doubt their own lived realities, leading to the normalization of gaslighting within relationships and perpetuating inequalities.

Toxic Masculinity and Gaslighting:

The construct of toxic masculinity, deeply embedded within society, can also serve as an accomplice to gaslighting. Men, socialized to suppress emotions and maintain dominance, may resort to gaslighting tactics to assert control over their female partners or peers. The perpetuation of societal expectations that suppress emotional expression fosters an environment that enables gaslighting practices to thrive, ultimately harming both men and women. It is crucial that we challenge these traditional masculine norms to create a culture that rejects gaslighting and fosters healthy emotional communication.

Intersectionality and Gaslighting:

An important aspect that society often overlooks when it comes to gaslighting is the intersectionality of one's identity. Individuals from marginalized backgrounds, such as racial or ethnic minorities, the LGBTQ+ community, or individuals with disabilities, often face higher rates of gaslighting due to societal power imbalances. This compounded form of gaslighting adds an extra layer of complexity, making it essential for society to acknowledge and address these different intersections of identity in the fight against gaslighting.

Education and Empathy:

To combat the silent acceptance of gaslighting within society, it is vital that we prioritize education and empathy. By incorporating anti-gaslighting curriculums in schools, workplaces, and public spaces, we can raise awareness about this insidious behavior and empower individuals to recognize and address gaslighting when they encounter it. Moreover, fostering empathy and compassion within our culture encourages individuals to develop healthier relationship dynamics, where gaslighting has no place.

Gaslighting thrives in a cultural landscape that inadvertently amplifies its effects. Society must confront the role it plays in perpetuating gaslighting behaviors, examine its norms, and actively dismantle the systems that enable this abuse. By challenging harmful narratives perpetuated by media, addressing rigid gender roles, embracing intersectionality, and prioritizing education, we can hope to create a society that is less tolerant of gaslighting, ultimately striving for healthier, more empathetic relationships for us all.

Recognizing Early Signs: Common Tactics and Red Flags

In the complex realm of human interactions, recognizing early signs of deception, manipulation, or harmful intentions can often be a daunting task. However, mastering the art of identifying common tactics and red flags is essential for protecting oneself and fostering healthier relationships. This chapter aims to shed light on the topic, exploring various strategies and providing real-life examples to sharpen your skills in detecting early signs of problematic behavior. By being vigilant and attentive, you can better navigate the intricate web of human interactions, whether in personal or professional settings.

Understanding the Influence of Nonverbal Communication

Nonverbal communication serves as a powerful tool in deciphering the intentions and emotions of individuals. Paying close attention to body language, facial expressions, and other nonverbal cues can provide valuable insights when assessing others' authenticity or intentions.

1. Inconsistencies in Body Language:

One of the most crucial early signs to watch out for is inconsistency in body language. For instance, if someone claims to be enthusiastic about a particular topic but fails to maintain eye contact, slouches, or engages in fidgeting, it may indicate a lack of genuine interest or discomfort.

2. Microexpressions:

Microexpressions, fleeting facial expressions lasting less than a second, can reveal true emotions that individuals may try to conceal. These brief displays of emotions, such as surprise, disgust, or contempt, can be indicative of contradictory feelings. Detecting these subtle cues can provide invaluable insight into someone's true intentions.

The Power of Verbal Cues

Apart from nonverbal communication, paying attention to the words someone uses and how they articulate them can also be instrumental in recognizing early signs of deception or manipulation.

1. Vague Statements:

Individuals who employ vague statements or use exaggerated language may be attempting to divert attention or manipulate a situation. For example, someone who frequently makes grandiose claims without providing concrete evidence may be lacking credibility.

2. Deflection and Omission:

Those with ulterior motives often practice deflection and omission as a means to avoid providing complete or transparent information. Red flags typically arise when individuals are reluctant to answer direct questions, change the subject abruptly, or selectively omit specific details.

Tactics of Manipulation and Deception

Manipulative individuals may resort to various tactics to achieve their desired outcomes. By recognizing these behaviors early on, you can shield yourself from becoming entangled in harmful interactions.

1. Gaslighting:

Gaslighting is a form of psychological manipulation that aims to make individuals doubt their own perceptions, memories, or sanity. This tactic is often employed by manipulating others into questioning their version of events, leading to confusion, self-doubt, and the erosion of an individual's self-confidence.

Example: Sarah's husband frequently denies incidents Sarah clearly remembers, leading her to question her sanity, ultimately giving him control over their relationship.

2. Love Bombing:

Love bombing involves showering someone with excessive attention, affection, and gifts during the early stages of a relationship, with the intent to gain control or manipulate them emotionally. This tactic creates a sense of dependency and can leave individuals vulnerable to subsequent manipulation.

Example: Mark bombards Sarah with constant attention and gifts, making her feel special and loved, but this is a ploy to gain control and undermine her autonomy.

Detecting Red Flags in Personal Relationships

Recognizing red flags in personal relationships can act as a safety net, allowing individuals to identify potentially toxic dynamics before they escalate.

1. Controlling Behavior:

One significant red flag is when an individual's behavior becomes increasingly controlling. Isolating someone from friends and family, dictating their routine, or frequently checking their whereabouts are all signs of an unhealthy level of control within a relationship.

Example: Emma's boyfriend starts insisting on knowing her every move, becoming irrationally jealous and isolating her from her friends, causing her to feel trapped and powerless.

2. Lack of Accountability:

Individuals who consistently refuse to take responsibility for their actions exhibit a red flag. They may engage in blame-shifting, denial, or manipulation tactics to avoid facing consequences, jeopardizing the trust within the relationship.

Example: Mike continuously blames others for his mistakes and refuses to acknowledge his own contribution, eroding trust and causing frustration within his personal relationships.

Recognizing Early Signs in Professional Situations

Identifying early signs of problematic behavior is equally crucial in professional settings. Recognizing these patterns can help individuals protect their interests and maintain a healthy work environment.

1. Microaggressions:

Microaggressions are subtle and often unintentional acts of discrimination or bias that can erode workplace morale and create a hostile environment. Recognizing these early signs is essential for fostering inclusivity and maintaining a fair and respectful workplace.

Example: Stephanie, an employee of color, constantly experiences her coworkers making dismissive comments about her culture, undermining her position and creating discomfort in the workplace.

2. Excessive Competitiveness:

While a healthy level of competition can motivate individuals, excessive competitiveness can damage teamwork and collaboration within a professional setting. Recognizing when competition becomes destructive allows for timely intervention and the preservation of a harmonious work environment.

Example: John consistently undermines his colleagues and takes credit for their work, creating a toxic and cutthroat work environment that hampers productivity and collaboration.

Recognizing early signs, common tactics, and red flags is a crucial skill for navigating the intricate world of human interactions. By paying attention to nonverbal cues, verbal patterns, and identifying manipulative tactics, individuals can protect their well-being, avoid harm, and foster healthier relationships. Vigilance, empathy, and an understanding of human behavior will empower you to navigate this complex web with greater confidence and authenticity.

Chapter 2: Psychological Underpinnings of Gaslighting

Gaslighting, a term derived from the 1944 film "Gaslight," refers to a psychological manipulation technique aimed at making the victim doubt their own perception of reality. It often involves the abuser distorting or rewriting facts, denying events, or even directly contradicting the victim's experiences. In this chapter, we will delve into the psychological underpinnings of gaslighting, exploring the mechanisms and motivations behind this insidious form of emotional abuse.

The Power of Perception:

To understand gaslighting, we must first examine the significance of perception in our lives. Each individual constructs their understanding of reality through their senses, experiences, emotions, and cognitive processes. However, our perceptions are not always accurate or reliable, as they can be influenced by biases, past experiences, and even physiological factors.

Perception is a complex interplay between the external world and our internal filters. Our brain interprets sensory information and ascribes meaning to it based on our existing beliefs, values, and expectations. While this process is generally adaptive and necessary for navigating the world, it also opens the door to manipulation and gaslighting.

Manipulation Techniques:

Gaslighters utilize a range of techniques to erode their victims' sense of reality and self-confidence. Let's explore some commonly employed tactics:

1. Undermining and Discrediting: Gaslighters systematically undermine their victims' beliefs, feelings, and experiences. They may mock their emotions or belittle their thoughts, implying their incompetence or unreliability. By challenging the validity of the victim's perception, the gaslighter slowly erodes their self-esteem and ability to trust themselves.

2. Confusion and Contradiction: Gaslighters employ confusion tactics to keep their victims off balance. They might repeatedly change their stance on an issue, creating inconsistency and making it difficult for the victim to maintain a clear understanding of reality. Over time, victims may doubt their own memory and become dependent on the gaslighter's version of events.

3. False Reinforcement: A gaslighter might intermittently reward their victim with compliments or acts of kindness, followed by harsh criticism or coldness. This inconsistent reinforcement confuses the victim, fostering a sense of self-doubt and heightened dependence on

the gaslighter for validation.

The Gaslighter's Motivation:

Understanding the motivations behind gaslighting allows us to explore the psychological underpinnings of this destructive behavior. While everyone has unique reasons for engaging in gaslighting, a deeper exploration uncovers common underlying psychological mechanisms:

1. Control and Power: Gaslighters often possess a strong need for control over others, deriving satisfaction from manipulating their victim's perception of reality. By seeking power over their victim's thoughts and emotions, they establish a sense of dominance and attain a feeling of superiority.

2. Insecurity and Self-Esteem: Gaslighters might have deep-rooted insecurities and low self-esteem. By undermining their victim's confidence, they alleviate their own feelings of inadequacy and gain a temporary ego boost. Unconsciously, they may perceive their victim's autonomy as a threat and employ gaslighting as a defense mechanism.

3. Projection: Gaslighters may project their own insecurities, flaws, or mistakes onto their victims. By diverting attention away from themselves and onto their victims, they avoid accountability and retain a sense of self-righteousness. This projection enables them to justify their actions and validate their distorted perspective.

Psychological Vulnerabilities:

Victims of gaslighting are not randomly chosen; gaslighters often target individuals with specific psychological vulnerabilities. Understanding these vulnerabilities sheds light on why some individuals are more susceptible to gaslighting than others:

1. Low Self-Esteem: Victims with low self-esteem are more likely to doubt themselves and seek approval from others. They are more susceptible to gaslighters who exploit their insecurities and reinforce their negative self-image.

2. Prior Trauma: Individuals with a history of trauma, abuse, or neglect may be more susceptible to gaslighting due to their heightened fear of retraumatization. Gaslighters capitalize on their victims' past experiences, leveraging them to create self-doubt and dependency.

3. Empathy and Compassion: People who possess high levels of empathy and compassion tend to give others the benefit of the doubt, making them easy targets for gaslighters. Their altruistic nature makes them more inclined to question their own perceptions and prioritize the well-being of the gaslighter over their own.

Understanding the psychological underpinnings of gaslighting is crucial in addressing this form of emotional abuse. By delving into the manipulative techniques, motivations, and vulnerabilities that contribute to gaslighting, we equip ourselves with the knowledge needed to recognize and counteract this destructive behavior.

As we move forward in this book, it is essential to continue exploring the complex dynamics of gaslighting and its impact on individuals and relationships. Only through this deeper understanding can we empower ourselves and others to break free from the grip of gaslighting and create healthier, more authentic connections.

Minds in Conflict: The Gaslighter's Psychopathology

Gaslighting is a form of psychological manipulation that aims to sow seeds of doubt in a targeted individual, making them question their own memory, perception, and sanity. It is a dark and insidious tactic that can have severe consequences on the victim's mental health and overall well-being. In this chapter, we will delve deeper into the disturbing psychopathology of gaslighters, seeking to understand the inner workings of their mind and the motivations that drive them to engage in such destructive behavior.

Understanding Gaslighting

Gaslighting is a term derived from the 1938 play "Gas Light" by Patrick Hamilton, which later became a film in 1944. The story revolved around a husband manipulating his wife by intentionally dimming the gas lights and denying having done so, causing her to question her sanity. This narrative serves as a poignant metaphor for the sinister tactics employed by gaslighters in real life.

Gaslighters exhibit a range of manipulative behaviors, often characterized by lying, denying, and trivializing the experiences and emotions of their victims. They create an environment of confusion and self-doubt, systematically eroding the victim's sense of reality.

By invalidating the victim's feelings and memories, gaslighters maintain control over their victims, who become increasingly dependent on their gaslighter for validation and guidance.

The Gaslighter's Profile

To understand the psychopathology of gaslighters, we must examine the characteristics that make them prone to engaging in this destructive behavior. Gaslighters often exhibit traits of narcissism, sociopathy, or psychopathy. They tend to possess a profound need for control, entertaining a grandiose sense of self-importance and an unwavering belief in their own superiority.

Gaslighters can be enigmatic and charming, capable of captivating others with their charisma and verbal prowess. They possess an uncanny ability to adapt their behavior to manipulate the thoughts and emotions of those around them, exploiting vulnerabilities to achieve their self-serving objectives. Behind this facade lies a profound and disturbing emptiness, unable to form authentic connections or empathize with others.

The Intricacies of Gaslighting

Gaslighting is a multifaceted process that involves several tactics aimed at undermining the victim's reality. Let us explore some of the most common strategies employed by gaslighters:

1. Denial and Rejection: Gaslighters often deny events, conversations,

or even promises, leading the victim to question their own memory or perception. This constant denial can create confusion and self-doubt, gradually eroding the victim's trust in their own judgment.

2. Counterfactual Manipulation: Gaslighters fabricate alternative versions of events, creating a distorted reality that aligns with their version of the truth. By doing so, they force their victims to question their own memories and perceptions, further reinforcing the gaslighter's desired narrative.

3. Trivialization and Emotional Invalidation: Gaslighters belittle the emotions, experiences, and concerns of their victims, diminishing their self-worth. By trivializing their emotions, gaslighters manipulate their victims into questioning their own feelings, further exacerbating the victim's already fragile state of mind.

4. Isolation: Gaslighters frequently isolate their victims from their support networks, making them increasingly dependent on the gaslighter for validation and emotional support. Through isolation, gaslighters solidify their control over their victims, leaving them susceptible to further manipulation.

The Psychological Toll

Gaslighting has severe psychological consequences for its victims. As gaslighters chip away at their reality and self-esteem, victims often experience feelings of confusion, anxiety, and depression. They wrestle with an overwhelming sense of self-doubt, unable to discern fact from fiction. This constant state of cognitive dissonance takes a toll on their mental health, leading to a range of long-term effects, including low self-esteem, difficulty trusting others, and even post-traumatic stress disorder (PTSD).

Breaking Free from Gaslighting

Recovering from gaslighting is a challenging journey that requires immense strength and self-reflection. Recognizing and acknowledging the gaslighter's manipulative tactics is the first step towards liberation. Victims must reestablish trust in their own perceptions and emotions, developing healthy coping mechanisms to counter the effects of gaslighting.

Seeking professional help, such as therapy, can greatly assist victims in their healing process. Therapists can provide a safe space for victims to explore their experiences, validate their emotions, and build resilience against further manipulation. Support groups and connections with other survivors of gaslighting can offer a sense of solidarity and empowerment, reassuring victims that they are not alone on their path to recovery.

Understanding the psychopathology of gaslighters is crucial in combating this insidious form of manipulation. By shedding light on their perverse motivations and tactics, we can empower victims to break free from the clutches of gaslighting and reclaim their sense of self. Continued research into the realm of gaslighting is essential to develop effective strategies to identify and confront these manipulative behaviors, ultimately promoting healthier and more supportive interpersonal relationships in our society.

Cognitive Dissonance: The Mental Struggle in the Victim

The human mind is a complex and intricate system, capable of incredible adaptability and resilience. However, when faced with conflicting beliefs or values, individuals often experience a state of mental tension known as cognitive dissonance. This chapter aims to explore the phenomenon of cognitive dissonance and its manifestation in victims of various circumstances, including abuse, manipulation, and deception. Through examining real-life examples and psychological theories, we will shed light on the struggle endured by those caught in the throes of cognitive dissonance.

Defining Cognitive Dissonance:

Cognitive dissonance, a term first introduced by psychologist Leon Festinger in 1957, refers to the state of psychological discomfort that arises when a person simultaneously holds two or more contradictory beliefs, ideas, or values. This discomfort compels individuals to alleviate the dissonance by modifying one or more of their beliefs, or by seeking out information that strengthens their existing beliefs. Victims of traumatic experiences, particularly those involving abuse, are susceptible to cognitive dissonance as they grapple with conflicting thoughts and emotions.

Cognitive Dissonance in Victims of Abuse:

Abuse, whether physical, emotional, or psychological, is an unfortunate reality that countless individuals endure. When victims form an emotional attachment or dependency on their abuser, they often experience cognitive dissonance as they reconcile their desire for safety and love with the painful reality of the abuse they endure. The mind grapples with a dissonant combination of love and fear, leaving victims trapped in an agonizing mental struggle.

Take, for example, the case of Sarah, a young woman who endured years of emotional manipulation in an abusive relationship. Despite her partner's recurrent verbally abusive behavior, Sarah found herself continually justifying his actions. She would convince herself that he truly loved her deep down or that his behavior was a result of stress. This cognitive dissonance enabled Sarah to continue believing in the compatibility of her partner's love while glossing over his abusive actions.

The Role of Sunk Costs:

A contributing factor to cognitive dissonance in victims is the concept of "sunk costs." Sunk costs refer to investments, be they emotional, financial, or otherwise, that individuals believe they cannot abandon without sacrificing their sense of self-worth or wellbeing. Victims may remain in abusive relationships due to the investments they have made in terms of time, energy, or even their own identity. Consequently, they engage in mental gymnastics, rationalizing their continued involvement despite the pain and suffering they experience.

The Manipulation of Reality:

Perpetrators of abuse often manipulate their victims' perception of reality, exacerbating the cognitive dissonance experienced by the victims. By distorting the truth or gaslighting their victims, abusers create an environment where victims question their own beliefs, memories, and sanity. This manipulation amplifies the internal struggle faced by victims, making it increasingly difficult to navigate their conflicting emotions and thoughts.

Cognitive Dissonance in Cases of Deception:

While cognitive dissonance is often associated with abuse, it also surfaces in cases of deception. Consider the infamous case of Bernie Madoff, a financial fraudster who orchestrated one of the largest Ponzi schemes in history. Many of Madoff's investors, despite harboring doubts about the legitimacy of their returns, chose to ignore warning signs in order to maintain their belief in the success of their investments. These investors experienced cognitive dissonance as they battled the conflict between their desire for financial gain and the unsettling realization that they had been deceived.

Self-Justification and the Reduction of Dissonance:

When faced with cognitive dissonance, individuals often engage in self-justification to alleviate the mental discomfort. Psychologists Elliot Aronson and Judson Mills developed a theory known as "effort justification," which suggests that people tend to value things more if they have had to work hard to attain them. Victims may employ this cognitive mechanism to justify their continued involvement in abusive relationships or deceptive situations. By convincing themselves that their suffering will eventually yield a positive outcome or that their abuser will change, victims attempt to reduce the dissonance they experience.

Cognitive Dissonance and Recovery:

Overcoming cognitive dissonance is a challenging journey for victims, one that often requires external support and professional intervention. Therapists and counselors play a vital role in assisting victims to recognize and navigate their conflicting beliefs and emotions, ultimately helping them break free from the shackles of cognitive dissonance. Encouraging victims to challenge their established beliefs and assumptions, therapists guide individuals towards embracing healthier cognitive frameworks, empowering them to rebuild their lives free from the influence of their abusers or deceivers.

Cognitive dissonance, a universal phenomenon, manifests profoundly in victims of abuse and deception. From the struggle between love and fear to the manipulation of reality, victims endure immense mental turmoil as they navigate conflicting thoughts and emotions. Acknowledging the prevalence and impact of cognitive dissonance is crucial in fostering empathy and understanding, ultimately promoting societal change and providing hope for those caught in the clutches of their own mental struggle.

The Cycle of Manipulation: Power Dynamics at Play

Power dynamics are an inherent aspect of human relationships, existing in personal, professional, and social spheres. Individuals strive to either gain power or preserve the power they hold, leading to the emergence of manipulative tactics that perpetuate and reinforce these power imbalances. In this chapter, we will explore the intriguing cycle of manipulation, examining how power dynamics drive manipulative behavior and contribute to the perpetuation of these unhealthy patterns. By delving into the various stages of manipulation, we aim to shed light on this complex phenomenon and empower readers to recognize and combat manipulation in their own lives.

Unveiling the Manipulative Cycle:

Manipulation is a multifaceted process that unfolds over several distinct stages, each fueling the next and creating a self-perpetuating cycle. By understanding these stages, we can decipher the intricate ways in which power dynamics are deployed and exploited.

1. Identification of Vulnerabilities:

The first stage of manipulation involves identifying the vulnerabilities and weaknesses of the potential target. Manipulators keenly observe their surroundings, seeking any signs of susceptibility that can be exploited for personal gain. These vulnerabilities could be emotional, financial, or based on the desire for acceptance or validation.

2. Establishing Trust and Control:

Once vulnerabilities are identified, the manipulator proceeds to establish trust and gain control over the target. This is often achieved through charm, flattery, or even deception. By creating a false sense of security and reliability, the manipulator prepares the groundwork for the further exploitation of power imbalances.

3. Exploiting Power Imbalances:

In this stage, the manipulator starts to exploit the power imbalances that exist within the relationship. These imbalances can be structural, such as those arising from differences in social status or hierarchies, or they can be psychological, stemming from a perceived need for approval or fear of rejection.

4. Emotional and Psychological Manipulation:

Having successfully established control and exploited power imbalances, the manipulator proceeds with emotional and psychological manipulation. This involves gaslighting, guilt-tripping, or using any other tactics that erode the target's confidence, autonomy, and mental well-being. By preying on insecurities and fears, the manipulator ensures their dominance over the target.

5. Maintenance and Reinforcement:

To perpetuate the cycle of manipulation, the manipulator must continuously maintain and reinforce their control. This can occur through reinforcement of power imbalances, psychological conditioning, or even direct threats. By keeping the target engaged and dependent, the manipulator cultivates an environment of control and submission.

Understanding Power Dynamics:

Key to unraveling the cycle of manipulation is recognizing the underlying power dynamics at play. Power can manifest in various ways, including physical, financial, social, or intellectual domains. Manipulation emerges when one individual uses their power or influence to shape and control another person's behavior or decisions.

In many cases, power imbalances are deeply rooted in societal structures and norms. Unequal distribution of power can be an outcome of gender, race, or economic disparities, making some individuals more prone to become manipulative or vulnerable to manipulation. It is vital to be cognizant of these dynamics in order to dismantle the cycle of manipulation and rectify systemic imbalances.

Breaking the Cycle:

Disentangling oneself from the manipulative cycle requires a conscious effort to reclaim power and assert independence. Recognizing the signs of manipulation, acknowledging one's vulnerabilities, and setting boundaries are essential steps towards breaking free from the grip of manipulation.

By fostering open communication, nurturing self-esteem, and cultivating healthy relationships, individuals can begin to dismantle power imbalances. Seeking support from friends, family, or professionals can significantly aid in overcoming the lingering effects of manipulation.

The cycle of manipulation is a deeply entrenched phenomenon that perpetuates unhealthy power dynamics in various aspects of our lives. By dissecting the stages of manipulation and understanding the power dynamics at play, we gain valuable insights into the intricacies of this complex issue.

However, recognizing manipulation is only the first step towards breaking free from its clutches. It is paramount that we actively work towards shifting power imbalances and fostering healthy relationships based on mutual respect and equality. Only then can we break the cycle of manipulation and create an environment that promotes authenticity, trust, and personal growth.

Attachment Theories and Gaslighting: Understanding Relational Foundations

In the realm of psychology, attachment theories and gaslighting are two critical concepts that shed light on the dynamics of relationships and the impact they have on individuals. Attachment theories delve into how early relationships shape our attachment styles, while gaslighting refers to a manipulative tactic employed by individuals to distort others' perception of reality. This chapter aims to explore the intricate connection between attachment theories and gaslighting, highlighting how early attachment experiences can contribute to vulnerability to gaslighting behaviors. Through a comprehensive discussion of research findings and real-life examples, we aim to provide readers with a deep understanding of the relational foundations underlying these concepts.

Attachment Theories: An Overview

Attachment theories were initially developed by British psychologist John Bowlby, who emphasized the significance of early attachment experiences between infants and their primary caregivers. Bowlby argued that these early relationships set the stage for how individuals form close bonds and navigate future interpersonal connections. He identified attachment as an innate instinct that ensures an infant's survival and emotional well-being. Bowlby's work paved the way for subsequent research on attachment styles, leading to the development of different attachment frameworks.

Mary Ainsworth, a developmental psychologist, expanded Bowlby's theories by introducing the concept of attachment styles through the strange situation experiment. This experiment aimed to assess an infant's behavior when separated from their caregiver and reunited under controlled conditions. Based on their observations, Ainsworth and her colleagues identified three primary attachment styles: secure, anxious-ambivalent, and avoidant.

1. Secure Attachment: Individuals with secure attachment styles tend to exhibit positive relationship experiences. They feel comfortable with intimacy, possess a positive self-image, and trust both themselves and others. They believe in their ability to navigate difficulties and seek support from their partners when needed.

2. Anxious-Ambivalent Attachment: This attachment style manifests in individuals who have a preoccupation with their relationships. They often fear abandonment, crave constant reassurance from their partners, and are overly sensitive to signs of rejection or criticism. They exhibit clingy behavior and may become engulfed in their relationships, leading to a cycle of emotional highs and lows.

3. Avoidant Attachment: Individuals with an avoidant attachment style tend to be emotionally distant and self-reliant. They fear intimacy and vulnerability, preferring to maintain independence within their relationships. Avoidantly attached individuals may

struggle with commitment and find it challenging to trust others fully.

Gaslighting: A Manipulative Game of Reality Distortion

While attachment styles provide insights into relationship dynamics, gaslighting delves into the ways individuals can manipulate others through deceptive tactics. The term "gaslighting" originated from the 1938 play "Gas Light" by Patrick Hamilton, which later inspired multiple movie adaptations. In the play, a husband manipulates his wife, making her question her own sanity by subtly manipulating her environment and experiences.

Gaslighting can occur in various forms, but it typically involves the manipulator destabilizing the victim's sense of reality, perception, and self-esteem. The manipulator employs tactics such as denial, misinformation, misdirection, and outright lies to create doubt in the victim's mind. Over time, this erodes the victim's self-confidence, leading them to rely heavily on the manipulator's version of events.

The Connection: Attachment Styles as Vulnerability Factors

In recent years, researchers have explored the connection between attachment styles and vulnerability to gaslighting behaviors. They argue that individuals with specific attachment styles may be more susceptible to gaslighting tactics due to their inherent relational tendencies. Understanding this connection is crucial for both mental health professionals and individuals seeking to protect themselves from gaslighting.

1. Secure Attachment and Gaslighting: Individuals with secure attachment styles are less likely to fall victim to gaslighting behaviors. Their ability to trust their perceptions and emotions provides a solid foundation from which to recognize manipulation early on. However, if subjected to persistent gaslighting tactics, even securely attached individuals can experience emotional distress and self-doubt.

2. Anxious-Ambivalent Attachment and Gaslighting: Anxiously attached individuals' inherent fear of rejection and preoccupation with their relationships make them vulnerable to gaslighting. Their excessive need for reassurance and fear of abandonment can lead them to question their own perceptions, making it easier for manipulators to exploit their vulnerabilities.

3. Avoidant Attachment and Gaslighting: Avoidantly attached individuals' discomfort with intimacy and reliance on self-reliance can make them attractive targets for gaslighters. Their fear of vulnerability and rejection may cause them to doubt their own experiences and emotions, enabling manipulators to gain control over their sense of reality.

Chapter 3: Personal Narratives and Gaslighting Experiences

Gaslighting is a term that emerged in the realms of psychology and sociology to describe a form of manipulation that seeks to undermine an individual's perception of reality. It is a subtle yet potent weapon that perpetrators use to gain power and control over their victims. In this chapter, we delve into personal narratives, shedding light on the various experiences of gaslighting and its profound impact on individuals' lives.

Gaslighting is a multidimensional concept, and its effects may vary widely depending on the specific circumstances and the vulnerability of the victim. To comprehend the intricacies of gaslighting, it is imperative to lend an ear to those who have endured its emotional turmoil firsthand. By hearing their voices, we can better understand the profound impact gaslighting has on one's perception, self-esteem, and overall well-being.

In this chapter, we present a collection of compelling personal narratives from individuals who have experienced gaslighting in diverse contexts. These captivating stories shed light on the complex dynamics at play, illustrating the insidious nature of gaslighting and the long-lasting scars it can leave behind.

Sophie's Story: A Slow, Pervasive Erosion

Sophie's tale starts innocuously enough, her gaslighting experiences beginning with subtle, barely noticeable manipulations. Her partner would frequently question her memory or portray her emotions as irrational, dismissing her concerns as mere overreactions. Initially, these tactics left Sophie second-guessing herself, gradually eroding her confidence and pushing her closer to the edge of her sanity.

Over time, it became apparent that Sophie's partner utilized gaslighting as a means of asserting dominance and control. He would twist the truth, deliberately distorting their shared memories, attempting to undermine her reality and replace it with his own twisted version. Sophie recalls vividly how she would doubt her own experiences and question her sanity, suffocating under the weight of self-doubt.

John's Journey: The Intersection of Gaslighting and Workplace Harassment

John's story takes us into the realm of workplace dynamics, where gaslighting can thrive too. A highly successful professional in his field, John believed his talents and contributions were valued by his colleagues. However, things took a turn when toxic office politics entered the picture.

John's boss, driven by jealousy and insecurity, employed a variety of gaslighting techniques to belittle his achievements and undermine his credibility. The boss specialized in subtly manipulating situations to cast doubt on John's competence and worth. Slowly but surely, John's self-assurance crumbled, and he found himself questioning his abilities and purpose in the workplace.

Diane's Experience: Gaslighting within Familial Relationships

Diane's narrative casts light on the somber reality that gaslighting can seep into the closest of relationships – familial bonds. Growing up in a dysfunctional family, Diane's parents leveraged gaslighting as a tool for control. Their constant denial of her valid feelings gaslit her into thinking that her emotions were unwarranted and invalid.

Diane's parents would twist the truth and manipulate her narrative, leading her to question her memories, feelings, and even her own identity. This insidious gaslighting eroded her sense of self-worth and inflicted lasting psychological trauma well into adulthood. Diane's heartbreaking story highlights the deep scars that can result from gaslighting within family structures.

Carla's Struggle: Escaping the Web of Gaslighting

In Carla's story, we witness the internal battle of an individual who has fallen victim to gaslighting but is determined to reclaim her reality. Carla's partner was a master manipulator, employing gaslighting techniques to exert control and authority over her life. The gaslighting tactics escalated over time, leaving Carla questioning her sanity and suppressing her own needs and desires.

However, Carla found strength in connecting with a support network and seeking therapy. Through this process, she gradually recognized the gaslighting for what it was – a deliberate attempt to undermine her sense of self. Armed with newfound awareness and self-belief, Carla eventually broke away from her toxic relationship, reclaiming her life and rebuilding her shattered self-esteem.

These personal narratives serve as invaluable testimonies to the pervasive and damaging effects of gaslighting. They unravel the intricate web of manipulation and control, shining a light on the psychological torture endured by its victims. By sharing these stories, we hope to give voice to those who have suffered in silence and foster a deeper understanding of gaslighting's far-reaching consequences.

Gaslighting is not limited to specific contexts or individuals. It permeates various aspects of human existence, leaving emotional scars that can persist long after the manipulation ceases. By bringing these narratives to the forefront, we aim to ignite conversations, challenge societal norms, and ultimately empower victims to break free from the suffocating grip of gaslighting.

As we conclude this chapter, we understand that personal narratives are just the beginning of understanding gaslighting fully. They lay the groundwork for exploring countermeasures, spreading awareness, and fostering a society that values truth, empathy, and self-expression.

Voices from the Shadows: Real Stories of Gaslighting Victims

In this chapter, we delve into the harrowing experiences of individuals who have fallen victim to the manipulative tactic known as gaslighting. Gaslighting is a psychological abuse tactic where one person seeks to gain power and control over another by making them question their reality, memories, and sanity. In our journey through the voices of these wounded souls, we aim to shed light on the devastating effects of gaslighting and provide solace and understanding to those who have lived in the shadows of this insidious manipulation technique.

Rachael's Story:

Rachael, a young and vibrant woman, had always been confident and self-assured. However, her life took an unexpected turn when she met Jeffrey, a charismatic and seemingly charming man. Little did she know that her encounter with Jeffrey would lead her down a dark and tumultuous path of gaslighting. Over time, Rachael noticed subtle changes in her reality; Jeffrey would frequently dismiss her opinions, manipulate her memory of events, and make her question her own sanity.

As the gaslighting intensified, Rachael faced a constant internal struggle between what she felt and what Jeffrey told her she should feel. This led to a deep sense of isolation and self-doubt that consumed her every waking moment. Rachael's story is a testament to the long-lasting emotional and psychological scars that gaslighting can leave on its victims.

Michael's Experience:

Michael, an intelligent and successful individual, found himself entangled in a toxic relationship with his former partner, Sarah. At first, Sarah appeared caring and loving, but as time went on, she began manipulating Michael's thoughts and emotions. She would ridicule his achievements, diminish his abilities, and consistently undermine his self-confidence. Slowly, Michael began questioning his own worth and capabilities.

In Michael's case, gaslighting had severe consequences not only on his self-esteem but also on his professional life. He found himself paralyzed by self-doubt, unable to perform at his job, and questioning his ability to make sound decisions. Sarah's relentless manipulation had left him feeling trapped and powerless, struggling to regain control of his own narrative.

Sarah's Struggle to Heal:

Sarah's journey towards healing began after escaping her gaslighting relationship. She realized the profound impact that her former partner's manipulation had on her sense of self. It took immense courage and strength for Sarah to confront the deep-seated self-doubt that had taken root within her.

Through therapy and support groups, Sarah learned to identify the signs of gaslighting, comprehend the strategies used by manipulators, and rebuild her self-esteem. She discovered that she was not alone in her struggles, and through connecting with other gaslighting survivors, she found solace and validation.

The Wider Impact:

Gaslighting does not only affect individuals in intimate relationships; it can permeate various aspects of one's life, including friendships, family relationships, and even work environments. Haley, for instance, shared her experience of being gaslighted by her close friend, Emma. Emma would consistently belittle Haley's achievements and portray her as incompetent, leaving Haley constantly questioning her abilities.

Moreover, gaslighting can extend to societal and larger-scale contexts. Communities and even entire nations can be gaslighted by leaders or institutions, manipulating public narratives, and gaslighting society as a whole. This manipulation technique can have far-reaching consequences on people's beliefs, trust, and overall well-being.

The stories shared in this chapter merely scratch the surface of the dark and damaging world of gaslighting. Gaslighting victims often silently suffer, their voices drowned out by doubt and confusion. By shedding light on their experiences, we hope to create a space where gaslighting survivors can find solace and support.

It is crucial for society as a whole to recognize gaslighting as a destructive abuse tactic and provide avenues for healing and recovery. Support networks, therapy, and education can play pivotal roles in restoring a gaslighting victim's sense of identity and providing them with the tools to rebuild their lives.

As we continue to explore the impact of gaslighting, it becomes increasingly evident that the shadows in which these individuals once resided need to be illuminated.

Only by listening to their voices, sharing their stories, and amplifying their experiences can we hope to create a world that stands against this manipulative and destructive tactic.

Patterns in Pain: Recurring Themes in Gaslighting Cases

Gaslighting, a term derived from the 1944 film "Gaslight," refers to a form of psychological manipulation wherein an individual, often a partner, attempts to distort another person's perception of reality, leading them to doubt their own experiences, memories, and sanity. Gaslighting is a grave abuse that leaves its victims wounded and perplexed, while the gaslighter gains power and control. This chapter delves into the intricate patterns observed in gaslighting cases, shedding light on the recurring themes that permeate these distressing experiences.

Invalidation of Feelings and Experiences:

One of the most prominent patterns in gaslighting cases is the systematic invalidation of the victim's feelings and experiences. Gaslighters deploy various tactics to undermine their victims' emotions, making them question the validity of their own reactions. Through dismissive phrases like "You're just being too sensitive" or "You're overreacting," gaslighters chip away at the victim's self-confidence, ultimately eroding their ability to trust their own emotions and instincts.

Distortion of Reality:

A fundamental aspect of gaslighting is the skillful manipulation of reality by the gaslighter. This pattern involves creating a parallel narrative that contradicts the victim's version of events, leaving them confused and uncertain. Gaslighters often revise or deny past conversations, events, or promises, painting the victim as unreliable or downright delusional. By gradually dismantling their perception of reality, gaslighters impose their own version of the truth, leaving the victim vulnerable and dependent on their gaslighter for a sense of stability.

Isolation and Alienation:

Gaslighters exploit their victims' vulnerabilities, often isolating them from friends, family, and support networks. This pattern serves to intensify the victim's dependence on the perpetrator, further cementing the gaslighter's control. The erosion of social connections can lead the victim to doubt their experiences, as they no longer have external sources to validate or challenge the gaslighter's narrative. This isolation creates a fertile ground for gaslighters to exert complete dominance over their victims' thoughts, feelings, and actions.

Blame-Shifting and Deflection:

Gaslighters possess a remarkable ability to absolve themselves of responsibility and shift blame onto their victims. This pattern is wielded as a weapon to deflect attention away from their own actions and maintain control over the narrative. By assigning fault to the victim for the gaslighter's behavior or planting doubts about the victim's sanity, the gaslighter skillfully avoids accountability, leaving the victim feeling guilty, confused, and constantly on the defensive.

Exploitation of Vulnerabilities:

Another recurrent theme in gaslighting cases is the exploitation of the victim's vulnerabilities. Gaslighters keenly identify and target areas of insecurity, often using them as leverage to manipulate their victims. Whether it be exploiting a history of mental health issues, past trauma, or personal insecurities, gaslighters use these vulnerabilities to gain power and control over their victims' emotions, thoughts, and decisions.

Reversal of Reality:

Gaslighters employ an unsettling technique of reversing roles and projecting their behaviors onto their victims. This pattern involves gaslighters accusing the victims of behaviors they themselves commit, leading to self-doubt and confusion. By painting themselves as the victims, gaslighters effectively distort the power dynamics and perpetuate the cycle of manipulation.

Gaslighting in Gender Dynamics:

While gaslighting can occur in any relationship, it is crucial to acknowledge its prevalence in gender dynamics. Gaslighting within romantic relationships often manifests as a method of consolidating power and control over women. Society's history of gender inequality and patriarchal norms create an environment where gaslighting is both enabled and normalized. Women are frequently subjected to gaslighting tactics aimed at undermining their autonomy, eroding their confidence, and enabling the perpetuation of power imbalances.

Patterns observed in gaslighting cases are crucial in understanding and tackling this prevalent form of psychological manipulation. By shedding light on these recurring themes, we hope to amplify awareness, empower victims, and equip society with the knowledge necessary to identify, intervene, and ultimately eradicate gaslighting. Breaking free from the chains of gaslighting requires a collective effort to support and validate the experiences of victims, challenge societal norms, and foster empathy and compassion in all facets of our lives.

Gaslighting Across Different Relationships: From Partners to Parents

Gaslighting is an insidious form of psychological manipulation, in which a person seeks to erode another individual's sense of reality and self-worth. It is a tactic commonly employed in various relationships, including romantic partnerships and parent-child dynamics. This chapter will explore the alarming prevalence of gaslighting and its detrimental impact on victims, shedding light on how this manipulation manifests differently across different relationships. By examining these patterns, we can develop a deeper understanding of the power dynamics at play and how to identify and combat gaslighting behaviors.

Understanding Gaslighting

To comprehend the phenomenon of gaslighting, it's essential to delve into its origins. The term "gaslighting" derives from a play titled "Gas Light" written by Patrick Hamilton in 1938, which was later adapted into two successful films. The plot revolves around a husband who manipulates his wife into questioning her reality, making her believe she is going insane. This concept gained traction as individuals recognized similar patterns in their own relationships.

The underlying element of gaslighting is emotional manipulation, which undermines the victim's perception of their own experiences. Perpetrators often use tactics such as denial, distortion, diversion, and minimization to exert control and foster self-doubt in their targets. Gaslighting is not exclusive to any particular relationship type and can occur between spouses, partners, parents, siblings, or even colleagues. In this chapter, we will primarily focus on the dynamics of gaslighting within romantic partnerships and parent-child relationships.

Gaslighting in Romantic Partnerships

Gaslighting in romantic partnerships can be devastating, as it chips away at the victim's self-esteem, confidence, and overall mental well-being. Initially, this manipulation may be subtle, making it difficult for victims to recognize. The gaslighter often showers the victim with love and affection, creating a sense of security and dependence.

Over time, the gaslighter may start to gradually introduce doubts, making the victim question their perception of reality. They may downplay or dismiss the victim's emotions, experiences, and even memories, causing the victim to second-guess themselves. The gaslighter may also manipulate the events and narratives, creating a distorted version of reality that serves their interests.

Gaslighters often exhibit controlling behavior, discouraging the victim from seeking external validation or support. They may isolate the victim from friends and family, making it easier to maintain control and assert dominance. Over time, victims of gaslighting begin to doubt their own judgment, relying solely on their gaslighting partner's perspective.

Recognizing the signs of gaslighting in romantic relationships is crucial, as it allows victims to break free from the cycle of manipulation. Common red flags include constantly feeling confused or disoriented, having difficulty making decisions, and constantly apologizing or second-guessing oneself. Victims may also experience feelings of anxiety, depression, or self-doubt, impacting their overall mental health.

Gaslighting in Parent-Child Relationships

Gaslighting can also occur within parent-child relationships, often driven by distorted power dynamics. Children rely on their parents for love, support, and guidance, making them particularly vulnerable to gaslighting tactics. In this context, gaslighting can have severe long-term effects on a child's development and self-esteem.

Parents engaging in gaslighting behavior may manipulate their children's perception of reality to maintain control or exert authority. They may dismiss or trivialize their child's emotions, labeling them as oversensitive or irrational. This invalidation of the child's emotions makes them doubt their own experiences, leading to potential psychological trauma.

Gaslighting parents may also play favorites among their children, pitting them against each other to assert control and create division.

By twisting events and facts, gaslighting parents can mold their children's memories and perceptions, leading to confusion and self-doubt.

Children who have experienced gaslighting from their parents may exhibit symptoms such as chronic self-doubt, difficulty trusting their own judgment, and feeling the need to constantly seek validation from others. These effects can carry into adulthood, impacting their personal relationships and hindering their ability to make independent decisions.

Gaslighting is a destructive manipulation tactic that occurs across various relationships, including romantic partnerships and parent-child dynamics. By understanding the different manifestations and consequences of gaslighting in these relationships, we can empower ourselves and others to identify and combat this harmful behavior.

Recognizing the signs of gaslighting is crucial to breaking free from its grip and rebuilding one's sense of self. Utilizing support systems and seeking professional help are essential steps in the healing process. By shedding light on gaslighting, we can create a society that holds accountability for manipulative behaviors, fostering healthier and more authentic relationships.

The Social Dimension: Group Gaslighting and Mob Mentality

In the realm of social interactions and human dynamics, there are fascinating phenomena that arise when individuals come together in groups. One such phenomenon, which has gained significant attention in recent years, is the concept of group gaslighting and mob mentality. This chapter aims to explore the intricacies of these social dynamics, shedding light on their origins, consequences, and potential countermeasures.

Understanding Group Gaslighting

To comprehend group gaslighting, it is essential to first understand gaslighting as an individual psychological manipulation tactic. Traditional gaslighting occurs when one person intentionally manipulates another's perception of reality, causing them to doubt their own sanity or judgment. Similarly, group gaslighting occurs when multiple individuals collectively engage in this psychological manipulation, leading a targeted individual, or even an entire society, to question their sanity, doubts, or beliefs.

Group gaslighting can often be observed in situations where a particular narrative or ideology becomes dominant within a group. The members of this group reinforce each other's beliefs, attempting to establish a collective reality that serves their purposes. Dissenting opinions or independent thought are often suppressed or discredited, leading to widespread conformity and agreement within the group.

Origins of Group Gaslighting

The origins of group gaslighting can be traced back to various underlying factors within human psychology and social dynamics. One key aspect is the innate human desire for validation and acceptance from others. People naturally seek approval and are more likely to adopt beliefs or opinions supported by their social circles. This tendency can lead to the formation of echo chambers, where members support each other's views, reinforcing their shared reality.

Furthermore, social identity theory plays a significant role in understanding group gaslighting. Humans tend to align themselves with various social groups and identities, forming a sense of belonging and an "us versus them" mentality. In an attempt to maintain cohesion within their group, individuals may resort to gaslighting tactics to discredit opposing opinions and reinforce collective beliefs.

Groupthink, a phenomenon coined by social psychologist Irving Janis, is closely related to group gaslighting. Groupthink occurs when members of a group prioritize consensus and harmony over critical thinking. This collective desire for agreement can lead to the suppression of dissenting voices and further facilitate the manipulation of reality.

Examples of Group Gaslighting

Throughout history, numerous examples demonstrate the effects of group gaslighting and its profound impact on society. A notable historical case study is the rise of Nazi Germany under Adolf Hitler. Hitler and his followers effectively employed group gaslighting tactics to manipulate the German population, promoting an ideology that ultimately resulted in immense suffering and tragedy.

During the period leading up to World War II, Hitler's Nazi regime strategically spread propaganda and suppressed dissenting voices to solidify their collective reality. By portraying Jewish people as the cause of Germany's problems, Hitler successfully manipulated public opinion and created an environment where German citizens questioned their previous values and moral compass. The result was an entire nation succumbing to group gaslighting, allowing atrocities to occur under the guise of a twisted collective reality.

Another noteworthy example can be seen in the advent of social media and online communities. Platforms like Twitter and Facebook have enabled the rapid dissemination of information and facilitated the formation of virtual groups. However, these online environments often promote group gaslighting, leading to the amplification of certain narratives while marginalizing dissenting opinions.

In recent years, social media has witnessed numerous instances of viral mob mentality, where a large group of individuals collectively attacks an individual or an idea, often without a proper understanding of the situation. This mob mentality perpetuates group gaslighting, as the overwhelming numbers and collective agreement can cause targeted individuals to doubt their own realities or opinions. The consequences of such incidents can be severe, often resulting in public shaming, career destruction, and emotional distress for the individuals involved.

Countering Group Gaslighting and Mob Mentality

While the power of group gaslighting and mob mentality is undeniable, it is essential to explore potential countermeasures. Whether at an individual or societal level, recognizing and addressing these dynamics is crucial for building healthier social structures.

Promoting critical thinking and independent thought is an integral part of countering group gaslighting. Encouraging individuals to question the dominant narratives and fostering an environment where dissenting opinions are respected can help prevent the formation of echo chambers and enable a more diverse exchange of ideas.

Media literacy programs and education are also effective tools in combating group gaslighting. By teaching individuals to critically analyze information, fact-check, and evaluate multiple perspectives, they become more resistant to manipulation and misinformation.

Furthermore, social media platforms themselves play a vital role in addressing group gaslighting and mob mentality. These platforms must be proactive in implementing strategies that promote healthy discussion, constructive disagreement, and responsible information sharing. Employing algorithms that prioritize diverse content and engaging users in conversations that expose them to opposing viewpoints can help counter the echo chamber effect.

Lastly, fostering empathy and understanding within society can mitigate the destructive power of group gaslighting. By actively encouraging open dialogue, empathetic listening, and respectful disagreement, individuals are more likely to form meaningful connections and challenge their own biases.

The social dimension of group gaslighting and mob mentality presents a complex and impactful phenomenon. Understanding its origins, recognizing its manifestations throughout history and in contemporary society, and exploring potential countermeasures are necessary steps toward creating a more informed and empathetic society. By addressing these dynamics head-on, we can build social structures that celebrate diversity, critical thinking, and respect for differing perspectives.

Chapter 4: Recognizing and Addressing Gaslighting in the Moment

Gaslighting is a manipulative tactic that aims to control and undermine someone's perception of reality. It can be an incredibly damaging form of psychological abuse, leading the victim to doubt their own thoughts, feelings, and experiences. Chapter 4 of this book will delve into recognizing and addressing gaslighting in the moment, offering practical strategies to empower individuals to identify and confront this insidious behavior.

Understanding the Dynamics of Gaslighting

To effectively combat gaslighting, it is crucial to comprehend its underlying dynamics. Gaslighters typically engage in a range of tactics, such as denying the victim's experiences, trivializing their emotions, and distorting facts. They aim to establish dominance and control over their victims, while at the same time creating an atmosphere of confusion and self-doubt.

Recognizing Gaslighting Behaviors

One of the primary challenges in confronting gaslighting is recognizing its presence. Gaslighters are often skilled at subtly manipulating situations and conversations, making it difficult for victims to identify the abuse. Chapter 4 will equip readers with tools to recognize gaslighting behaviors, such as invalidation, deflection, and the creation of false narratives. By highlighting these tactics, individuals can develop a heightened awareness and better protect themselves against gaslighting.

Trusting Your Perception of Reality

Gaslighting effectively undermines an individual's trust in their own perception of reality. Victims begin to question their thoughts, feelings, and memories, often feeling confused and disoriented. This chapter will explore strategies to regain confidence in one's perception, emphasizing the importance of self-trust and validation. By learning to trust their intuition, victims can begin to break free from the gaslighter's constraints and reclaim their sense of reality.

Interrupting the Gaslighting Cycle

Addressing gaslighting in the moment requires a combination of assertiveness and emotional intelligence. This chapter will provide practical techniques for interrupting the gaslighting cycle, such as setting clear boundaries, using "I" statements to express emotions and experiences, and maintaining a calm but assertive demeanor.

These strategies will empower victims to challenge the gaslighter's manipulation and regain control over their own narrative.

Building a Support Network

Gaslighters often isolate their victims, cutting them off from supportive relationships and external perspectives. Recognizing this, Chapter 4 underscores the importance of building a strong support network that can provide validation, guidance, and empathy. Surrounding oneself with trusted friends, family, or professionals who understand the dynamics of gaslighting can be instrumental in countering the effects of gaslighting in the moment.

Educating Others about Gaslighting

While it is essential to address gaslighting on an individual level, it is equally important to educate others about this form of abuse. Chapter 4 emphasizes the role of education in raising awareness, encouraging readers to speak up about gaslighting and its consequences. By sharing personal experiences or advocating for increased public understanding, individuals can contribute to a collective effort to combat gaslighting and protect potential victims.

Self-Care in the Face of Gaslighting

Gaslighting takes a toll on one's emotional well-being, often leading to anxiety, depression, and a loss of self-esteem. Chapter 4 stresses the significance of self-care as a means of resilience building.

Readers will learn various self-care strategies, such as mindfulness practices, engaging in hobbies, seeking therapy, and practicing self-compassion. These techniques can help victims maintain their mental and emotional health while navigating the challenging process of addressing gaslighting.

Celebrating Progress and Reflecting on Growth

Recognizing and addressing gaslighting is a journey that requires time and effort. Chapter 4 promotes self-reflection by encouraging readers to celebrate their progress, no matter how small, as they work towards healing and reclaiming their sense of self. Acknowledging personal growth and achievements provides motivation and reinforces the resilience needed to confront gaslighting in the moment.

Chapter 4 has explored the dynamics of gaslighting, its devastating impact, and effective strategies to recognize and address gaslighting behaviors in real-time. By understanding the manipulative tactics, boosting self-trust, interrupting the gaslighting cycle, building a strong support network, advocating for awareness, practicing self-care, and celebrating progress, victims can reclaim their reality and break free from the control of gaslighters.

Remember, recognizing gaslighting is the first step towards regaining control over your own life. By honing your understanding of gaslighting tactics and implementing the strategies discussed in this chapter, you can begin to dismantle the power that gaslighters hold over you. Let this chapter be a guide on your journey towards healing, empowerment, and personal growth.

Grounding Techniques: Staying Connected to Reality

In our fast-paced and unpredictable world, it is increasingly common for individuals to feel disconnected, overwhelmed, or lost in their thoughts. The constant bombardment of information and stimuli can make it challenging to stay present and engaged with the world around us. However, there are several effective grounding techniques that can help us reconnect with reality and find inner balance. In this chapter, we will explore these techniques, their benefits, and how they can be incorporated into our daily lives.

Understanding Grounding

Grounding, in essence, is the practice of bringing your awareness back to the present moment and connecting with the physical world. It involves redirecting your attention away from distressing thoughts, anxieties, or overwhelming emotions and focusing on the here and now. Grounding techniques are particularly useful for managing anxiety, stress, and dissociation, as they help individuals stay centered and present in their immediate surroundings.

The Power of the Senses

One of the most effective ways to ground ourselves is by engaging our senses. Our senses provide invaluable feedback about our environment, helping us foster a deeper connection with reality.

Here are some techniques that harness the power of the senses:

1. Five Senses Check-In: Begin by sitting or standing comfortably, and take a moment to notice what you can see, hear, smell, taste, and touch. Observe the colors, shapes, and movements in your visual field, listen closely to the sounds around you, identify any aromas or scents present, savor the flavors in your mouth, and feel the textures beneath your fingertips. This exercise allows your mind to anchor in the present moment.

2. Barefoot Walking: Walking barefoot on natural surfaces such as sand, grass, or even cool tiles can be incredibly grounding. As you walk, pay attention to the sensation on the soles of your feet, the change in textures, and the connection with the earth. This technique not only provides a sense of physical grounding but also fosters a deeper connection with nature.

3. Sensory Exploration: Take a few moments each day to engage in sensory exploration. Pick up objects and explore their textures, smells, and weight. Try new foods and savor their flavors and aromas. Engage in activities that allow you to tune into your senses, such as creating art, gardening, or playing a musical instrument. The more we engage our senses, the more present and connected we become.

Connecting with the Breath

Our breath is a powerful tool that can anchor us in the present moment. When we are stressed or anxious, our breathing becomes shallow and rapid, often leaving us feeling disconnected. By mindfully focusing on our breath, we can reestablish a sense of calm and connectedness. Here are a few techniques to help you connect with your breath:

1. Belly Breathing: Find a comfortable position, either sitting or lying down, and place one hand on your abdomen. Take a slow, deep breath in through your nose, allowing your belly to rise as you fill your lungs with air. Exhale slowly through your mouth, feeling your belly fall. Repeat this breathing pattern several times, focusing solely on your breath and the sensation it creates in your body.

2. Counting Breath Technique: Close your eyes and begin to count your breaths. Inhale deeply, counting "one," then exhale fully. As you continue breathing, count each exhale, starting from one and working your way up to ten. Once you reach ten, start over again. This technique allows your mind to focus on the breath and stay grounded in the present moment.

3. Breath Awareness Meditation: Set aside a few minutes each day to engage in breath awareness meditation. Find a quiet space, close your eyes, and bring your attention to your breath. Notice the sensation of air entering and leaving your nostrils, the rise and fall of your chest, and the rhythm of your breathing. Whenever your mind starts to wander, gently bring it back to your breath. This practice not only helps ground you but also cultivates mindfulness and enhances overall well-being.

Grounding Objects and Anchors

Sometimes, we need external tools to help us ground ourselves in reality. Grounding objects or anchors can serve as physical reminders of our connection to the present moment. Here are a few examples:

1. A Special Item: Choose an object that holds personal significance to you, such as a pebble from a favorite beach or a piece of jewelry passed down from a loved one. Carry this item with you or place it somewhere visible as a grounding reminder. When you touch, hold, or look at it, allow yourself to fully connect with the present moment and the memories associated with the object.

2. Visualization Techniques: Close your eyes and imagine a calming and grounding scene, such as a peaceful forest or a serene beach. Engage all your senses to make the visualization as vivid as possible. By visualizing these grounding scenes, you can tap into their calming and centering qualities, even when you're unable to physically be in them.

3. Tactile Stimulation: Incorporate the use of tactile objects into your grounding routine. Squeeze stress balls, hold smooth stones, or use textured fabrics. Engaging in tactile stimulation provides sensory input that can help you reconnect with reality and find comfort during moments of distress.

Practicing grounding techniques is essential for maintaining a healthy connection with reality in our often overwhelming and hectic modern lives. By engaging our senses, reconnecting with our breath, and utilizing grounding objects, we can cultivate a strong foundation that allows us to navigate life's challenges with greater ease. Incorporate these techniques into your daily routine, and relish in the profound benefits of staying grounded in the present moment.

Conversational Aikido: Defusing Gaslighting Tactics

In the realm of interpersonal communication, there are moments when we encounter individuals who employ manipulative tactics to gain power and control within conversations. One such technique that sinister individuals often use is gaslighting. Gaslighting is a form of psychological manipulation that sows seeds of doubt, confusion, and self-doubt in the victim, making them question their own perceptions, memories, and even reality. This chapter aims to provide you with insights into the art of "Conversational Aikido," a metaphorical approach to neutralizing gaslighting tactics and protecting ourselves from emotional harm.

Understanding Gaslighting:

To effectively combat gaslighting, we must first understand its intricacies. Gaslighting operates by exploiting a person's trust and belief in others, creating a sense of uncertainty and dependency. The term "gaslighting" originates from the 1938 play "Gas Light" by Patrick Hamilton, which tells the story of a husband deliberately manipulating his wife's reality to drive her to insanity. In today's world, gaslighting exists in various contexts, such as personal relationships, friendships, workplaces, and even on social media.

Identifying Gaslighting Tactics:

Gaslighters employ a wide range of tactics to undermine their victims' confidence and distort their sense of reality. By recognizing these tactics, one can better defend against them. Here are some common gaslighting techniques to watch out for:

1. Denial and Contradiction: Gaslighters often deny having said or done something, even in the face of overwhelming evidence. They may also contradict statements they previously made, making the victim question their own recollection of events.

2. Misdirection: Gaslighters often change the subject or redirect blame, steering the conversation away from their own actions. Through misdirection, they seek to control the narrative and evade accountability.

3. Minimization and Belittlement: Gaslighters downplay the victim's emotions or experiences, making them feel insignificant or irrational. This tactic aims to diminish the victim's feelings and discredit their perspectives.

4. Projection: Gaslighters may accuse the victim of the very behavior they are exhibiting, projecting their faults onto the victim. By doing so, they redirect attention and alleviate themselves of responsibility.

5. Creating Doubt and Confusion: Gaslighters intentionally create situations that leave the victim uncertain or confused. By

manipulating the victim's perception of reality, they can maintain control over the conversation.

Conversational Aikido: Defusing Gaslighting Tactics:

Just as in the martial art of Aikido, which emphasizes using an opponent's energy against them, Conversational Aikido involves redirecting the gaslighter's tactics to defuse their manipulative agenda. It requires building awareness, cultivating emotional intelligence, and adopting effective communication strategies. Let's explore some techniques that can help us master Conversational Aikido:

1. Validate Your Own Reality: Gaslighters rely on their victims doubting themselves and feeling unsure about their memories or perceptions. By affirming your own experiences and trusting your judgment, you build resilience against their tactics.

Example: "I respect that your opinion differs from mine, but I am confident in my understanding of the situation."

2. Seek External Validation: When gaslighting makes you doubt your own sanity, reach out to trusted friends, family members, or professionals who can offer an objective perspective. Their validation can help you maintain a firm grip on reality.

Example: "I'm feeling unsure about what happened. Can I get your opinion on this situation?"

3. Set Clear Boundaries: Establishing and communicating clear boundaries conveys that you will not tolerate gaslighting behavior. Clearly state what is acceptable and unacceptable to you, ensuring that gaslighters understand the consequences of their actions.

Example: "I will no longer engage in discussions where my experiences are disregarded or twisted. Respectful communication is essential for our relationship."

4. Respond with Calm and Confidence: Gaslighters thrive on emotional reactions. By remaining calm, composed, and confident, you deny them the emotional power they seek. Redirect their attention to the facts and evidence at hand.

Example: "I understand you have a different perspective, but let's focus on the facts. Here's the evidence to support my point of view."

5. Use the Power of Questions: Skillfully asking strategic questions can challenge a gaslighter's narrative and make them accountable for their actions. Thought-provoking questions expose inconsistencies and force them to critically evaluate their behavior.

Example: "Can you help me understand why you constantly contradict what you said before? It's confusing, and I'd like to gain clarity."

6. Document Key Events: Keeping a record of incidents, conversations, and their outcomes can serve as a reality check. This

practice provides concrete evidence that helps you maintain clarity and avoid becoming entangled in gaslighting traps.

Example: "In our previous conversation on [date], you mentioned [details]. Can you explain why your perspective has changed now?"

Mastering the art of Conversational Aikido equips us with the skills needed to defuse gaslighting tactics effectively. By understanding gaslighting, identifying its tactics, and employing the techniques of Conversational Aikido, we can protect ourselves from emotional harm and reclaim our sense of reality. Remember, maintaining a strong sense of self, seeking external validation, setting clear boundaries, responding with calm and confidence, using strategic questions, and documenting key events are powerful tools in the face of gaslighting. Armed with these skills, you can navigate conversations with a renewed clarity, ensuring your emotional well-being remains intact.

Establishing Boundaries: Preventing Further Manipulation

In our lives, we often come across individuals who possess a knack for manipulation - those skilled in the art of bending others to their will. Whether it be in personal relationships, the workplace, or even within our social circles, these manipulators have mastered the art of getting what they want while ignoring the needs of others. Recognizing their tactics and learning to establish boundaries is crucial for maintaining our well-being and preventing further manipulation. In this chapter, we will explore the various strategies and techniques to effectively establish boundaries and protect ourselves from the harmful effects of manipulation.

Understanding Manipulation

Manipulation is not a new phenomenon, nor is it limited to a particular group or society. It is a complex combination of psychological and behavioral tactics employed to assert control and influence over others for personal gain. Recognizing manipulation is the first step in establishing healthy boundaries. Manipulators are often charismatic, charming, and skilled at exploiting vulnerabilities in their targets. They use various techniques such as gaslighting, guilt-tripping, emotional blackmail, and even physical intimidation to achieve their goals.

Recognizing Manipulative Behavior

To establish boundaries effectively, it is essential to be able to identify manipulative behavior. While there is no foolproof method to detect every manipulator, there are some common signs to watch out for. Manipulators tend to be highly persuasive, adapt their behavior to suit their interests, and often thrive on the weaknesses of others. They may project a persona that gives off an initial air of trustworthiness but maintains a lack of genuine empathy towards others.

Additionally, manipulative individuals often employ deceitful tactics, such as constantly lying, excessively flattering others, playing the victim card, or using emotional manipulation to control their targets. They may create an atmosphere of fear or dependency, making it difficult for victims to break free from their clutches. By observing, paying attention, and trusting our instincts, we can develop a keen sense of discernment to recognize manipulative behavior when we encounter it.

The Consequences of Succumbing to Manipulation

Before examining how to establish boundaries, it is crucial to understand the consequences of continuously allowing manipulation to persist in our lives. Succumbing to manipulation not only undermines our autonomy and self-esteem but can also have significant long-term effects on our mental health and overall well-being. The emotional toll can range from anxiety and depression to a lack of confidence and constant doubt in our decision-making abilities. By allowing manipulation to thrive unchecked, we inadvertently grant manipulators power over our lives, leaving us feeling helpless and trapped.

Establishing Boundaries

Establishing boundaries is an essential element of self-preservation when dealing with manipulation. It empowers us to assert our needs, protect our emotions, and maintain control over our lives. However, creating boundaries can be easier said than done. Many factors, such as fear, guilt, or a desire to please others, often hinder our ability to set and maintain boundaries effectively. Nevertheless, with awareness and practice, we can equip ourselves with the tools to establish boundaries that prevent further manipulation.

1. Self-Awareness

The first step towards establishing boundaries is developing self-awareness. This involves understanding our own values, beliefs, needs, and desires. By having a clear sense of self, we become less susceptible to manipulation because we can identify when our boundaries are being violated. Reflect on your personal boundaries, what is acceptable to you and what is not. This introspection will serve as a foundation for creating boundaries that align with your core values.

2. Identify Manipulative Behavior

Learning to recognize manipulative behavior is crucial in establishing effective boundaries. By identifying the tactics employed by manipulators, we can respond appropriately and protect ourselves. Keep an eye out for signs of gaslighting, guilt-tripping, or emotional manipulation. Trust your intuition, and if something feels off, take a step back and reassess the situation. Remember, you have the power to choose how you want to be treated and whether to engage with manipulators or disengage to protect your well-being.

3. Communicate Assertively

Clear and assertive communication is vital when setting boundaries. Express your needs, expectations, and limits openly and without ambiguity. Be assertive but respectful, making it clear that your boundaries are non-negotiable. Practice using "I" statements to express your feelings and desires, avoiding generalizations or accusing language. For instance, instead of saying, "You always manipulate me," try saying, "I feel manipulated when XYZ happens, and I am not comfortable with that."

4. Consistency and Follow-Through

Consistency is key when dealing with manipulative individuals. Once you have set your boundaries, it is crucial to follow through with them. Inconsistent behavior can give manipulators an opportunity to exploit any perceived weakness. Stay firm, and don't cave in to guilt or pressure. Though manipulation may escalate when confronted with boundaries, maintaining your resolve sends a clear message that you cannot be manipulated any longer.

5. Seek Support

Building and maintaining boundaries can be a challenging task, especially when dealing with persistent manipulation. Seek support from trusted friends, family, or professionals who can provide guidance and validation. Having a support network strengthens your resolve to establish and maintain boundaries while ensuring you don't feel isolated or alone in your journey.

Establishing boundaries is an ongoing process that requires self-awareness, assertiveness, and consistency. By recognizing manipulative behavior, communicating effectively, and seeking support, we reclaim control over our lives, protect our emotional well-being, and prevent further manipulation. Remember, setting boundaries is not an act of selfishness but an act of self-preservation. Embrace your right to establish boundaries, and confidently navigate a life free from manipulation.

Chapter 5: Healing the Psychological Wounds of Gaslighting

In this chapter, we will delve into the complex process of healing the psychological wounds inflicted by gaslighting. Gaslighting is a form of psychological manipulation that undermines a person's sense of reality and self-worth, leaving lasting scars on their psyche. Understanding the impact of gaslighting and developing strategies to heal is vital for those who have experienced this insidious form of abuse.

Gaslighting: A Traumatic Deception

Gaslighting is a term derived from the 1944 film "Gaslight," where the protagonist's husband systematically manipulates her into doubting her own sanity. This psychological tactic extends far beyond the realm of cinema, as many individuals have experienced the devastating effects of gaslighting in their personal relationships.

Gaslighting takes many shapes and forms, but its core elements remain consistent. The gaslighter employs tactics such as constant lying, minimizing or denying their actions, blame shifting, and manipulation to manipulate the victim's perception of reality. Over time, the victim begins questioning their own sanity, memory, and judgment, leading to profound psychological trauma.

Recognizing the Pain: Identifying the Wounds

Healing begins with acknowledging the emotional wounds inflicted by gaslighting. Victims often struggle to recognize the extent of the damage, especially when the gaslighter succeeds in undermining their self-confidence and trusting instincts. Common emotional wounds include anxiety, depression, low self-esteem, feelings of worthlessness, and an overarching fear of trusting oneself or others.

The journey to healing necessitates developing self-awareness, understanding the dynamics of gaslighting, and unraveling the impact it has had on one's psychological well-being. With time and a supportive environment, the wounded can gradually regain their sense of self and autonomy.

Unraveling the Gaslighting Web: Therapy and Support

Therapy plays a crucial role in the healing process for gaslighting victims. A therapist provides a safe and non-judgmental space to explore and unravel the deeply ingrained beliefs and trauma caused by gaslighting. Individual therapy, such as cognitive-behavioral therapy (CBT) or dialectical behavior therapy (DBT), can help victims reframe distorted beliefs, develop healthier coping strategies, and rebuild their self-esteem.

Group therapy or support groups offer an additional layer of healing for gaslighting survivors. Sharing experiences with others who have endured similar psychological manipulations creates a sense of validation and solidarity. In these groups, individuals can both receive and offer support, fostering a community of healing and growth.

Rebuilding Trust and Self-Confidence

Gaslighting shatters one's ability to trust oneself and others. Recovering from the trauma of gaslighting requires active efforts to rebuild trust and restore self-confidence. Mindfulness practices and self-compassion exercises are powerful tools in this process.

By practicing mindfulness, individuals learn to stay present in the moment, enhancing their ability to recognize and challenge the gaslighter's attempts to undermine their sense of reality. Additionally, fostering self-compassion allows victims to acknowledge their pain, embrace their strengths, and nurture their wounded inner selves.

Reclaiming Power: Assertiveness and Boundaries

Gaslighting victims often experience a pervasive sense of powerlessness and a lack of control over their own lives. To heal, it becomes crucial to reclaim personal power and establish healthy boundaries.

Assertiveness training empowers individuals to advocate for their needs, opinions, and boundaries effectively. Learning to communicate assertively helps victims regain their voice and establish healthier dynamics in their relationships. Recognizing and setting clear boundaries paves the way for safer connections and reduces the likelihood of falling prey to future gaslighting attempts.

Redefining Identity: Finding Self again

Gaslighting manipulates victims into doubting their own identity. Rediscovering oneself after gaslighting involves comprehensive self-reflection, self-expression, and rebuilding an authentic sense of self. Journaling, creative outlets, and self-exploration activities help reconnect with one's true desires, values, and passions. Engaging in activities that bring joy and a sense of fulfillment can provide a roadmap to self-discovery and rebuilding a solid foundation of identity.

Healing from the psychological wounds of gaslighting requires time, self-compassion, and a supportive network. This chapter aimed to shed light on the various aspects of healing, including recognizing the emotional wounds, seeking therapy and support, rebuilding trust and self-confidence, reclaiming personal power through boundaries and assertiveness, and redefining one's identity.

Recovering from gaslighting is a deeply personal journey, and while the path may be challenging, it is important to remember that healing is possible. Armed with self-awareness, therapeutic interventions, and a commitment to self-growth, gaslighting survivors can reclaim their lives, rebuild their self-esteem, and cultivate relationships grounded in trust and authenticity.

Rebuilding Self-Trust: Steps to Regain Confidence

Self-trust is an integral aspect of personal growth and development. When we trust ourselves, we have faith in our abilities, decisions, and judgments, enabling us to navigate life with confidence and resilience. However, certain experiences and circumstances can damage our self-trust, leaving us feeling uncertain and doubtful. If you find yourself grappling with a lack of self-trust, fear not! This chapter will explore effective steps to help you rebuild your self-trust and regain the confidence needed to live a fulfilling and empowered life.

Acknowledging the Loss:

The first step towards rebuilding self-trust is recognizing and acknowledging that it has been compromised. Take a moment to reflect on the situations or experiences that may have contributed to this loss. Was there a particular event or relationship that shook your confidence in yourself? Identifying the source of your doubts and insecurities will provide a foundation upon which you can begin your journey towards rebuilding self-trust.

Practice Self-Compassion:

Rebuilding self-trust requires a compassionate approach towards yourself. Understand that everyone makes mistakes and experiences setbacks at some point in their lives. Instead of berating yourself for past errors, offer yourself forgiveness and understanding. Treat yourself with the same kindness and compassion you would extend to a dear friend. Remember, self-compassion is not about avoiding accountability but recognizing that you are human and deserving of forgiveness.

Cultivate Self-Awareness:

Developing self-awareness is crucial in the process of rebuilding self-trust. Take the time to explore your thoughts, emotions, and beliefs without judgment. Awareness allows you to identify patterns of behavior that may be contributing to your lack of trust in yourself. This can include questioning your self-talk, examining the origin of your doubts, and recognizing any limiting beliefs that may be holding you back. By cultivating self-awareness, you gain valuable insights to guide you towards rebuilding self-trust.

Set Realistic Expectations:

Setting unrealistic expectations for yourself can erode your self-trust. Acknowledge that you are a work in progress and that growth takes time and effort. Avoid comparing yourself to others, as everyone's journey is unique. Instead, focus on your own progress and celebrate the small wins along the way. By setting realistic expectations, you create a supportive environment for self-trust to flourish.

Challenge Negative Thoughts:

Negative thoughts and self-doubt can be major obstacles when it comes to rebuilding self-trust. Challenge these thoughts by asking yourself if there is any evidence to support them. Often, our negative thoughts are based on assumptions or past experiences that are no longer relevant. If you find yourself ruminating or engaging in self-sabotaging behaviors, consciously shift your focus towards positive affirmations and intentions. Gradually, this practice will help rewire your thinking patterns and foster trust in yourself.

Take Small Steps:

Rebuilding self-trust is a journey that requires patience and consistency. Focus on taking small steps towards regaining your confidence rather than attempting to overhaul everything at once. Break down your goals into manageable tasks and accomplish them one by one. By achieving these smaller milestones, you build evidence of your abilities and reinforce your self-trust along the way.

Seek Support:

Rebuilding self-trust can be challenging, but you don't have to do it alone. Seek support from trusted friends, family members, or even a therapist. Share your struggles and aspirations with someone who can offer guidance, encouragement, and a fresh perspective. Sometimes, an external viewpoint can help you uncover aspects of yourself that you may have overlooked. Engaging with a supportive network can provide invaluable emotional support throughout your journey of rebuilding self-trust.

Practice Self-Reflection:

Self-reflection is a powerful tool when it comes to rebuilding self-trust. Set aside regular time for introspection and journaling. Write down your thoughts, fears, and aspirations. This process allows you to gain clarity on your values, strengths, and weaknesses. Through self-reflection, you will gradually rediscover your true self and deepen your connection with your intuition. Trusting your instincts is a fundamental aspect of rebuilding self-trust, and self-reflection serves as a conduit to harness this inner wisdom.

Practice Self-Trust Daily:
Rebuilding self-trust requires consistent practice. Commit to engaging in activities that help you develop self-trust on a daily basis. This may involve setting healthy boundaries, saying no when necessary, and making decisions that align with your values. Prioritize self-care and engage in activities that nourish your mind, body, and soul. By consistently demonstrating trust in yourself through your actions, you will gradually rebuild and strengthen your confidence.

Rebuilding self-trust is a transformative process that requires time, effort, and self-compassion. By following the steps outlined in this chapter, you will embark on a journey towards regaining your confidence and living a fulfilling life based on trust in yourself. Remember, rebuilding self-trust is a personal and unique experience. Embrace the journey, celebrate your progress, and have faith that you possess the strength and resilience to reclaim your self-trust.

Therapeutic Interventions: Seeking Professional Guidance

In the fast-paced and challenging world we live in, it is not uncommon for individuals to face various emotional, psychological, and behavioral difficulties. Whether it be coping with everyday stressors, managing a mental health condition, or navigating through significant life changes, seeking professional guidance through therapeutic interventions can be a transformative and empowering experience. This chapter explores the importance of seeking professional guidance, the various therapeutic interventions available, and the benefits they bring to individuals' overall well-being.

1. Understanding the Need for Professional Guidance

1.1 Acknowledging Personal Challenges

Life can present us with a myriad of challenges, such as relationship issues, job-related stress, grief, trauma, or chronic mental health conditions. It is essential to recognize when we require additional support to navigate these challenges effectively. Seeking professional guidance is a proactive step towards improving our mental health and overall quality of life.

1.2 Breaking Down Stigma

Historically, seeking professional guidance has been stigmatized, often associated with weakness or personal failure. However, contemporary society is gradually dismantling these outdated beliefs. Mental health awareness initiatives and increasing acceptance of therapy have cultivated a more positive and inclusive environment, encouraging individuals to seek the help they need without fear of judgment.

1.3 Benefits of Seeking Professional Guidance

By opting for professional guidance, individuals gain access to expertise, knowledge, and strategies offered by qualified mental health professionals. Therapeutic interventions provide a safe and confidential space to explore and understand personal challenges, develop coping mechanisms, and foster personal growth. Seeking professional guidance is an investment in oneself, promoting a stronger sense of self-awareness, resilience, and well-being.

2. Therapeutic Interventions: The Range and Scope

2.1 Psychotherapy

Psychotherapy, also known as talk therapy, is one of the most commonly sought therapeutic interventions. It involves engaging in conversations with a trained therapist to explore emotions, thoughts, and behaviors. Psychotherapy can be offered in various modalities, including individual, group, family, or couples therapy, depending on the nature and requirements of the individual's concerns.

2.2 Cognitive-Behavioral Therapy (CBT)

CBT is a specific type of psychotherapy that focuses on exploring the connections between one's thoughts, feelings, and behaviors. By identifying and challenging negative and irrational thoughts, CBT helps individuals develop healthier thinking patterns. This intervention is highly effective in treating various mental health conditions such as anxiety, depression, and phobias.

2.3 Dialectical Behavior Therapy (DBT)

DBT is an evidence-based form of therapy primarily used to treat individuals struggling with borderline personality disorder, self-harm behaviors, and difficulties in emotion regulation. DBT combines elements of cognitive-behavioral therapy with mindfulness techniques, helping individuals achieve emotional balance and develop effective coping strategies.

2.4 Acceptance and Commitment Therapy (ACT)

ACT is a mindfulness-based therapy that emphasizes accepting distressing thoughts and feelings while committing to goal-directed behavior aligned with personal values. By developing psychological flexibility, individuals learn to adapt to life's challenges while maintaining a sense of purpose and fulfillment.

2.5 Eye Movement Desensitization and Reprocessing (EMDR)

EMDR is a specialized therapy frequently used to treat individuals experiencing trauma-related disorders, post-traumatic stress disorder (PTSD), and disturbing memories. By engaging in bilateral stimulation, typically through eye movements, individuals can process traumatic memories, reduce distress, and restore a sense of emotional well-being.

2.6 Art Therapy

Art therapy harnesses the expressive power of art and creative processes to promote emotional healing and personal growth.

Through various artistic mediums, individuals can explore their emotions, enhance self-expression, and gain insight into their unconscious thoughts and conflicts. Art therapy is often used in conjunction with traditional psychotherapy to complement the therapeutic process.

2.7 Mindfulness-Based Interventions

Mindfulness-based interventions, such as mindfulness-based stress reduction (MBSR) and mindfulness-based cognitive therapy (MBCT), incorporate meditation practices and awareness of the present moment to reduce stress, enhance well-being, and cultivate self-compassion. These interventions are particularly beneficial in managing anxiety, depression, and chronic pain.

3. The Benefits of Professional Guidance

3.1 Improved Self-Awareness

Therapeutic interventions provide individuals with an opportunity to gain deep insights into their thoughts, emotions, and behavioral patterns. By enhancing self-awareness, individuals can better understand the root causes of their difficulties and take steps towards personal growth and self-improvement.

3.2 Enhanced Coping Skills

The acquisition of effective coping strategies is a significant benefit of seeking professional guidance. Therapists equip individuals with practical tools and techniques to manage stress, regulate emotions, and navigate life's challenges more effectively. These coping skills can promote resilience and contribute to improved overall well-being.

3.3 Strengthening Relationships

Through therapeutic interventions, individuals can explore their relationship patterns, improve communication, and cultivate healthier connections with others. This process enhances personal relationships, family dynamics, and professional interactions, leading to a richer and more fulfilling social life.

3.4 Increased Emotional Resilience

Professional guidance fosters emotional resilience by helping individuals develop healthier ways of managing and expressing their emotions. By learning to identify and regulate emotions, individuals can navigate difficult situations with increased confidence and emotional stability.

3.5 Empowerment and Personal Growth

By actively engaging in therapeutic interventions, individuals cultivate a sense of empowerment, taking charge of their mental health and personal growth. Therapists act as guides, facilitating individuals' exploration of their own strengths, values, and goals, ultimately leading to a more fulfilling and purposeful life. Therapeutic interventions offer a wealth of benefits for those seeking professional guidance. By acknowledging personal challenges, breaking down stigma, and embracing the range of therapeutic approaches available, individuals can embark on a transformative journey towards improved well-being, self-understanding, and personal growth. As society continues to recognize the value of seeking professional support, the path to mental health and overall wellness becomes more accessible and inclusive to all.

Affirmation and Validation: The Role of Support Systems

Chapter 1: The Power of Affirmation

In our journey through life, we often encounter challenges and obstacles that can sometimes leave us feeling discouraged, doubtful, and lacking confidence. During such moments, having a support system that provides affirmation becomes crucial. Whether it is in our personal relationships, academic or professional pursuits, or even our own self-belief, the power of affirmation can significantly impact our well-being and overall success.

Defining Affirmation:

Affirmation can be described as the act of acknowledging and validating one's feelings, thoughts, and experiences in a positive and meaningful way. It involves offering genuine praise, support, and encouragement to someone, emphasizing their strengths and abilities, and helping them build self-confidence. Affirmation can be provided by individuals or by support systems such as family, friends, mentors, and even professional networks.

The Importance of Affirmation:

Affirmation plays a vital role in shaping our identity and helping us navigate the challenges we face. It acts as a catalyst for personal growth, as it enables us to believe in ourselves, our abilities, and our potential. When we receive affirmation, it reinforces our self-worth, empowering us to overcome obstacles, pursue our goals, and embrace new opportunities.

Affirmation and Emotional Well-being:

Affirmation impacts our emotional well-being in profound ways. When we feel affirmed, our self-esteem improves, reducing feelings of insecurity, anxiety, and self-doubt. It fosters a positive mindset and helps us develop an optimistic outlook on life. Affirmation also bolsters our resilience, enabling us to bounce back from setbacks with renewed determination and strength.

Affirmation and Relationships:

In the realm of interpersonal relationships, affirmation plays a central role. When we feel affirmed by our loved ones, it strengthens our bond, fostering trust and respect. Affirmation nurtures a sense of belonging and validates our emotions and experiences, creating a supportive environment where we can openly express ourselves without fear of judgment. Being affirmed also enhances our ability to empathize with and support others, strengthening the fabric of our relationships.

Affirmation and Personal Growth:

Affirmation is closely intertwined with personal growth. It propels us out of our comfort zones and encourages us to explore our potential. When we receive affirmation, we are more likely to take risks, try new things, and expand our horizons. This leads to personal development as we uncover hidden talents, develop new skills and interests, and ultimately, discover our true selves.

Chapter 2: The Impact of Validation

Validation goes hand-in-hand with affirmation, providing further support to individuals navigating the complexities of life. It is a fundamental aspect of any support system, enhancing the bonds of trust and understanding between individuals. Validation, much like affirmation, contributes significantly to personal growth, emotional well-being, and the overall success of individuals.

Defining Validation:

Validation refers to the act of recognizing, accepting, and understanding another person's emotions, thoughts, and experiences. It involves acknowledging their perspectives, beliefs, and reactions without judgment or invalidation. Validation creates a safe space for individuals, validating their emotions and helping them feel seen and understood.

Validation and Emotional Well-being:

Similar to affirmation, validation plays a crucial role in nurturing emotional well-being. When we feel validated, it affirms that our emotions are legitimate, normal, and acceptable. This acknowledgment helps us develop a healthy understanding of our feelings and reduces any shame or self-disapproval we may experience. Validation also encourages emotional expression, allowing us to process and cope with challenging situations effectively.

Validation and Relationships:

In the context of relationships, validation is foundational to building trust and deeper connections. When we validate others, we demonstrate empathy, compassion, and respect for their experiences. This fosters an environment of open communication, where individuals can express themselves freely without fear of rejection or criticism. Validation strengthens relationships by creating a sense of safety, leading to increased intimacy and mutual understanding.

Validation and Self-Validation:

While external validation is crucial, self-validation is equally important. Self-validation involves recognizing and accepting our own emotions and experiences without seeking approval from others. It empowers us to trust our intuition, beliefs, and capabilities. Cultivating self-validation allows us to develop self-esteem and resilience, reducing our dependence on external validation alone.

Chapter 3: Building an Effective Support System

An effective support system is essential for providing affirmation and validation. Building and maintaining such a system requires intentional effort from both individuals seeking support and those offering it. This chapter explores the key elements necessary for creating a robust support system that fosters affirmation and validation.

Mutual Trust:

Trust forms the foundation of any supportive relationship. Individuals must feel secure in confiding their fears, dreams, and vulnerabilities without the fear of betrayal or judgment. Building trust within a support system involves demonstrating reliability, integrity, and the willingness to empathize and support in times of need.

Effective Communication:

Open and honest communication is vital for both individuals seeking support and those providing it. The ability to express emotions and concerns freely enables both parties to feel heard and understood. Active listening, non-judgmental responses, and empathy facilitate effective communication within a support system.

Recognizing Boundaries:

Respecting boundaries is crucial in any support system. Individuals must be aware of each other's needs, limitations, and personal space. Establishing and maintaining healthy boundaries ensures that the support provided is focused, respectful, and appropriate.

Regular Check-ins:

Providing ongoing support requires regular check-ins to assess the well-being and progress of individuals within the support system. These check-ins provide opportunities for affirmation, validation, and adjustments to better meet the evolving needs of the individuals involved.

Encouraging Growth:

A healthy support system empowers individuals to grow and pursue their goals. Encouragement, guidance, and constructive feedback are necessary to help individuals overcome challenges and expand their potential. The support system should serve as a catalyst for personal growth and development.

Chapter 4: The Ripple Effect of Support

A robust support system not only benefits individuals directly involved but also has a cascading effect on their interactions with others. The impact of affirmation and validation extends beyond the immediate support system, positively impacting personal relationships, work environments, and society as a whole.

Impact on Personal Relationships:

When individuals feel affirmed and validated within their support system, they carry that positivity into their personal relationships. They are better equipped to communicate openly, empathize with others, and provide affirmation and validation to their loved ones. This ripple effect strengthens the foundation of relationships, creating a culture of support and understanding.

Impact on Work Environments:

Affirmation and validation also have a profound impact on work environments. When individuals feel valued and validated, they are more likely to exhibit higher job satisfaction, motivation, and productivity. Supportive work environments foster innovation, collaboration, and growth, leading to increased employee well-being and organizational success.

Impact on Society:

Finally, the impact of affirmation and validation extends to society at large. When individuals experience empathy, authenticity, and affirmation within their support systems, they are more likely to exhibit these qualities in their interactions with others. This creates a culture of compassion, understanding, and support, which in turn leads to stronger communities and a more harmonious society.

Journaling through the Journey: The Healing Power of Writing

In this fast-paced world filled with constant distractions and chaos, it has become increasingly challenging to find moments of solace and introspection. Our minds are often cluttered with a multitude of thoughts, anxieties, and worries that hinder our ability to connect with ourselves and find inner peace. However, through the art of journaling, we can embark on a transformative journey that allows us to heal, grow, and rediscover ourselves. In this chapter, we will delve into the healing power of writing, exploring how journaling can be a powerful tool for self-reflection, emotional release, and personal growth. Let us embark on this journey together and unravel the profound connection between pen, paper, and the human spirit.

Section 1: The Cathartic Release of Emotions

The human experience is fraught with a wide range of emotions, some pleasant and uplifting, while others are painful and burdensome. While we often suppress or ignore these emotions, they continue to linger within us, affecting our mental and emotional well-being. Journaling provides an outlet for this emotional baggage, offering a safe space to express and process our feelings. By putting thoughts and emotions onto paper, we create distance between ourselves and our internal struggles, gaining clarity and perspective on our experiences.

When we journal, we grant ourselves permission to be vulnerable, allowing our deepest fears, disappointments, and joys to come to the surface. This act of emotional release can be incredibly cathartic, providing relief from the weight we've been carrying. Through journaling, we give ourselves the freedom to feel our emotions fully, letting go of any shame or judgment that may have held us back. By unburdening our hearts and minds onto the pages of our journal, we can begin to heal wounds and nurture our emotional well-being.

Section 2: Self-Reflection and Personal Growth

In the hustle and bustle of daily life, it is easy to lose sight of our personal growth and the lessons we've learned along the way. Journaling acts as a mirror, allowing us to reflect on our experiences, thoughts, and actions. By writing down our thoughts, we gain insight into our patterns, behaviors, and beliefs. This retrospective examination opens up opportunities for self-improvement and growth.

Through journaling, we can identify recurring patterns or unhealthy habits that may hinder our progress. By recognizing these patterns, we empower ourselves to make positive changes and take steps towards personal transformation. Moreover, journaling helps us set goals, track our progress, and celebrate our achievements, however small they may seem.

Section 3: Finding Serenity in the Chaos

Life can be overwhelming at times, and it is easy to get caught up in the chaos of our daily routines. Journaling offers an escape from this tumultuous external world, providing a sanctuary of tranquility within the pages of our journals. When we dedicate time to write, we create a sense of stillness and presence, fostering a deeper connection with ourselves and the present moment.

Within the solitude of journaling, we find a space where we can reconnect with our dreams, aspirations, and innermost desires. As we pour our thoughts onto paper, the noise of the outside world fades, and we become attuned to our true essence. Journaling allows us to rediscover our passions, values, and purpose, reminding us of what truly matters in our lives.

Section 4: Cultivating Gratitude and Mindfulness

In a society that often fixates on what is lacking rather than what is present, journaling serves as a gentle reminder to cultivate gratitude and mindfulness. Through the act of writing, we acknowledge and appreciate the small joys and blessings in our lives, no matter how insignificant they may seem. Keeping a gratitude journal allows us to shift our perspective towards the positive, fostering a sense of inner contentment and appreciation.

In addition, journaling is a gateway into the practice of mindfulness, the art of being fully present in the here and now. As we write, we become more attuned to our thoughts, sensations, and surroundings. Each stroke of the pen becomes a mindful act, allowing us to savor the process rather than merely focusing on the end result. With mindful journaling, we unlock the potential for greater self-awareness, acceptance, and a deeper connection to the world around us.

Section 5: Enhancing Mental and Emotional Well-being

Journaling has been shown to have numerous benefits for our mental and emotional well-being. Studies have shown that expressive writing can reduce symptoms of anxiety, stress, and depression. By externalizing our thoughts through writing, we gain a new perspective on our challenges, allowing us to reframe our experiences and reduce their emotional impact.

Furthermore, journaling provides an opportunity to process traumatic events or difficult emotions that may have been suppressed or unexpressed. Through the act of writing, we can untangle the knots in our minds, learning to make sense of our experiences and find meaning in the face of adversity. As we navigate our way through the pages of our journals, we discover our resilience, gaining a greater sense of control over our emotional well-being.

In the realm of journaling, we embark on a journey of self-discovery, healing, and personal growth. Through the act of writing, we allow ourselves to be vulnerable, releasing pent-up emotions and unburdening our hearts. Journaling encourages self-reflection, fostering personal growth and transformation. It provides a sanctuary of tranquility, enabling us to find solace amidst the chaos of life.

By cultivating gratitude and mindfulness, writing becomes a practice of contentment and presence. Lastly, journaling enhances our mental and emotional well-being, promoting resilience and greater control over our lives.

As we conclude this chapter, let us acknowledge the profound connection between writing and the human spirit. May we all embrace the healing power of journaling, and may the pages of our journals bear witness to our growth, dreams, and triumphs on this beautiful journey called life.

Chapter 6: Rebuilding Relationships after Gaslighting

Gaslighting is a form of psychological manipulation that aims to make the victim question their own reality, memory, or perception. It is a deeply damaging experience that can leave individuals feeling confused, isolated, and distrustful of others, especially those close to them. So, how does one heal and rebuild relationships after enduring gaslighting? In this chapter, we will explore the nuanced process of rebuilding relationships in the aftermath of gaslighting, highlighting the importance of self-care, communication, and trust.

Understanding the Impact of Gaslighting

Gaslighting can inflict severe emotional wounds that can take time to heal. The gaslighter's constant manipulation and invalidation of the victim's thoughts, feelings, and experiences can erode their self-esteem and lead them to doubt their own judgment. As a result, relationships can become strained or even broken beyond repair.

1. Begin with Self-Care

Before embarking on the journey of rebuilding relationships, it is crucial to prioritize self-care. Gaslighting often creates a sense of self-doubt and leaves individuals feeling vulnerable and emotionally depleted. Therefore, taking time to heal and focus on self-nurturing activities is essential for rebuilding a strong foundation.

Engaging in activities that bring you joy, practicing self-compassion, and seeking therapy or support are vital steps in the healing process. By prioritizing your well-being, you will regain strength and clarity, enabling you to approach rebuilding relationships with a healthier mindset.

2. Recognize and Re-establish Boundaries

During the gaslighting experience, boundaries may have been blurred or disregarded altogether. It is necessary to re-establish and communicate your boundaries clearly. This step is crucial not only for your healing but also for rebuilding mutual trust within relationships.

Setting boundaries can include explicitly stating what behaviors you find unacceptable, as well as communicating your emotional needs. Be assertive when expressing your boundaries, and don't be afraid to ask for respect and understanding from those around you. Remember, it is your right to establish boundaries that promote your well-being.

3. Foster Open and Honest Communication

Rebuilding relationships requires open and honest communication.

However, after experiencing gaslighting, communication skills may have been undermined. It is essential to develop effective communication strategies to express your feelings, thoughts, and concerns assertively.

Consider using "I" statements when discussing difficult subjects. For example, instead of saying, "You always made me doubt myself," try saying, "I felt unsure about my own judgment during that time." This approach emphasizes your experience rather than pointing fingers, enabling a more constructive dialogue.

In addition, actively listen to the other person's perspective. Validate their feelings and experiences, and strive to understand their point of view. Effective communication means creating a space where both parties can be heard and respected.

4. Rebuilding Trust Gradually

One of the most challenging aspects of healing from gaslighting is rebuilding trust. Gaslighting erodes trust, leaving victims feeling skeptical and vulnerable. Rebuilding trust will take time, patience, and consistent effort from both parties involved.

Start by engaging in small, trust-building activities. Commit to following through on your promises and being reliable. Similarly, if you have been the victim of gaslighting, it is crucial to allow yourself to trust and be open to others gradually. Surround yourself with supportive and trustworthy individuals who can help rebuild your sense of security.

5. Seek Professional Help if Needed

Rebuilding relationships after gaslighting can be an intricate and challenging process, requiring professional guidance at times. Experienced therapists can provide specialized support, offering insights, strategies, and tools to navigate relationships and aid healing.

Therapy sessions may focus on healing past wounds, learning healthy coping mechanisms, and developing effective communication skills. Remember, seeking professional help is a courageous step towards regaining control of your life and rebuilding relationships in a healthy and sustainable way.

Rebuilding relationships after enduring gaslighting is a multifaceted journey that demands self-care, open communication, and patience. Gaslighting causes significant damage, shaking the very foundations of trust and security. However, with dedication and willingness from all parties involved, it is possible to restore relationships and move forward.

Remember, healing takes time and effort. Prioritize self-care, establish clear boundaries, communicate openly, and seek professional help if needed. Rebuilding relationships is a delicate process, but one that can lead to stronger, healthier connections built on trust, understanding, and respect.

Deciding to Stay or Leave: Navigating Difficult Decisions

Life is full of difficult choices, and one of the most challenging decisions we may face is whether to stay in a situation or leave it behind. Be it a job, a relationship, or a place we call home, the question of staying or leaving can be riddled with uncertainty, fear, and conflicting emotions. In this chapter, we will explore the intricacies of this decision-making process and delve into various factors that can help us navigate through these difficult choices. By understanding the complexities involved and examining different perspectives, we can gain clarity and make more informed decisions.

Examining the Inner Dialogue:

When faced with a challenging decision, it is often helpful to explore our thoughts and emotions regarding the situation. It is essential to engage in an inner dialogue and understand the reasons behind our desire to stay or leave. This introspection allows us to identify our fears, aspirations, and priorities that are influencing our decision.

Amidst the turbulence of emotions, it is crucial to remember that change, whether staying or leaving, can be discomforting. Our minds naturally gravitate towards familiarity and the known, even if it is not necessarily in our best interest. Recognizing this bias allows us to evaluate our situation more objectively.

Evaluating the Pros and Cons:

To gain clarity, it is vital to compile a list of the pros and cons of staying or leaving. This exercise assists in comprehensively understanding the implications of both choices, which in turn helps us make a decision that aligns with our values and goals.

When assessing the pros of staying, it is essential to consider factors such as stability, comfort, familiarity, and potential for growth or improvement. Conversely, when evaluating the cons of staying, one must analyze potential stagnation, missed opportunities, and any negative impacts on overall well-being.

Similarly, when examining the pros of leaving, ponder on factors like personal growth, new experiences, and potential for positive change. On the other hand, while analyzing the cons of leaving, consider aspects such as uncertainty, potential risks, and the emotional toll it might take.

Understanding our Values:

In the face of challenging decisions, understanding our values is paramount. Our values act as guiding principles, steering us in the direction that aligns with who we are and what we prioritize.

Reflecting on our core values allows us to evaluate whether our current situation resonates with those values. For example, if personal growth, autonomy, and creativity are high on our list of values, remaining in a stifling job where those values are not upheld may feel incongruent. Conversely, if stability, security, and loyalty are our priorities, leaving a stable job to pursue a riskier venture may not align with our values.

Considering External Factors:

While internal reflections and evaluations are crucial, considering external factors can also play a significant role in our decision-making process. These external factors primarily involve the influence of social support, financial considerations, and potential ramifications on our relationships.

Social support, such as family, friends, or mentors, can offer valuable insights and perspectives. Discussing our dilemma with trusted individuals can provide new angles and help us gain clarity about our decision.

Financial factors should also be considered, as they can significantly impact our ability to sustain ourselves or support our dependents. Evaluating the financial implications of staying or leaving can play a defining role in shaping our decision.

Furthermore, we need to be mindful of how staying or leaving may affect our relationships. It is important to consider the impact on our loved ones, as our decision can intimately affect their lives as well.

Striking a balance between our own needs and the needs of those around us is integral to making responsible decisions.

Listening to Our Intuition:

While rational analysis and assessments are valuable, our decisions should also be informed by our instincts and intuition. Sometimes, our gut feeling can guide us towards the right path, even when it defies logical reasoning.

Listening to our intuition involves tapping into our inner wisdom and allowing it to guide us towards what feels right. This requires honing our ability to tune in and trust ourselves, even when the external factors may tempt us to ignore our inner voice.

Deciding to stay or leave is an immensely difficult and personal choice. It requires immense introspection, evaluating pros and cons, considering our values, analyzing external factors, and listening to our intuition. However, there is no one-size-fits-all answer to this decision. What may be right for one person may not be the same for another.

The key is to remain compassionate towards ourselves while navigating this complex decision-making process. Acknowledge that it can take time and include periods of uncertainty and doubt. By exploring our inner dialogue, evaluating various factors, and listening to our intuition, we can pave the way for better decision-making and find greater fulfillment in our lives.

Rebuilding Trust with Others: Steps for Restoration

Trust is the foundation of any meaningful relationship, be it personal or professional. It is a fragile yet essential element that allows individuals to fully engage and rely on one another. However, trust can easily be damaged or broken, leading to a breakdown in communication and connection. In this chapter, we will explore the steps for restoring trust with others after it has been compromised. We will journey through a comprehensive process that can help mend broken bonds and rebuild trust, fostering healthier and stronger relationships.

Step 1: Acknowledge the Breach of Trust

The first and most crucial step in rebuilding trust is acknowledging that it has been broken. Denying or avoiding the breach of trust only prolongs the process of healing and recovery. It is essential to confront the issue head-on, taking responsibility for one's actions or being willing to address the actions of others. Avoiding blame games and instead focusing on understanding the impact of the breach is pivotal in laying the groundwork for restoration.

Step 2: Reflect on the Reasons

Once the breach of trust has been acknowledged, it is beneficial to reflect on the reasons behind it. Was there a lack of communication or a misunderstanding? Did conflicting priorities or personal insecurities play a role? By deeply reflecting on the circumstances that led to the breach, individuals can develop a deeper understanding of themselves and others. This self-awareness promotes personal growth and paves the way for more effective resolutions.

Step 3: Apologize and Seek Forgiveness

Apologies hold immense power when it comes to rebuilding trust. A sincere and heartfelt apology demonstrates accountability, remorse, and a genuine desire for reconciliation. To effectively apologize, one must first acknowledge the specific harm caused by their actions, express sincere regret, and demonstrate a commitment to making amends. Simultaneously, seeking forgiveness from the harmed individual allows them to have a voice in the healing process, promoting dialogue and understanding.

Step 4: Communicate Openly and Honestly

Open and honest communication is the cornerstone of trust restoration. Transparently sharing thoughts, feelings, and concerns fosters an environment of trust and vulnerability. It is essential to address any lingering doubts, fears, or questions that may arise during the rebuilding process. Similarly, listening attentively to the other person's perspective, without judgment or interruption, is vital in building mutual understanding and respect.

Step 5: Demonstrate Consistency and Reliability

To regain trust, it is crucial to demonstrate consistency and reliability in both words and actions. Empty promises or inconsistent behavior can further erode trust and hinder the rebuilding process. Instead, individuals must align their actions with their words, keeping commitments and follow through on promises. Consistency creates a stable foundation from which trust can grow again.

Step 6: Establish Boundaries and Expectations

Rebuilding trust can sometimes necessitate the establishment of new boundaries and expectations. Clearly defining personal boundaries, discussing expectations, and setting mutually agreed-upon guidelines ensure that all parties involved are on the same page moving forward. Having these guidelines in place allows everyone to feel secure and promotes a healthy and respectful relationship built on trust.

Step 7: Patience and Time

Rebuilding trust takes time and patience. It is crucial to recognize that trust cannot be instantly restored but rather grows gradually over time. Rushing the process may lead to further disappointment or frustration. Consistently demonstrating trustworthiness and remaining understanding of the hurt individual's healing process is vital. Patience allows the space needed for healing wounds, rebuilding confidence, and nurturing trust.

Step 8: Seek Professional Help if Necessary

In some cases, rebuilding trust may require the assistance of a trained professional, such as a therapist or mediator. These professionals can provide guidance, facilitate healthy communication, and offer strategies to overcome complex trust issues. Seeking help when needed should be seen as a proactive step towards rebuilding trust and strengthening the relationship.

Step 9: Learn from the Experience

Every relationship is an opportunity for personal growth and learning. In the process of rebuilding trust, it is important to reflect on the experience and identify lessons learned. Recognizing patterns that led to the breach of trust can help prevent similar occurrences in the future. By growing from the experience, individuals can enhance their understanding of themselves and others, fostering healthier relationships moving forward.

Step 10: Celebrate Progress

As trust is gradually restored, it is essential to celebrate the progress made along the way. Rebuilding trust can be challenging, and recognizing the efforts and growth achieved by both parties can reinforce the positive trajectory. Taking the time to celebrate small victories and acknowledging the hard work put into rebuilding trust can strengthen the bond and foster a deeper sense of connection.

Rebuilding trust with others is a courageous and transformative journey. It requires individuals to confront their vulnerabilities, take responsibility, and actively participate in the restoration process.

By following the steps outlined in this chapter, individuals can lay the foundation for rebuilding trust, fostering healthier, more resilient relationships. Remember, trust is a delicate flower that, once broken, needs care, patience, and nurturing to bloom once again.

Healthy Relationships 101: Traits of Respectful Interactions

In the journey of life, one of the most significant aspects that contribute to our happiness and well-being is healthy relationships. Whether they are with our family members, friends, romantic partners, or colleagues, the quality of our interactions greatly impacts our overall satisfaction in life. Developing a deep understanding of what constitutes a healthy relationship and cultivating the traits of respectful interactions can improve not only the quality of our relationships but also our own personal growth.

In this chapter, we will explore the key traits of respectful interactions and how they contribute to fostering and maintaining healthy relationships. By understanding and implementing these traits in our daily lives, we can create a positive and harmonious environment for ourselves and those around us.

1. Communication:

Effective and respectful communication is the very foundation of any healthy relationship. It involves actively listening to others, expressing ourselves clearly and honestly, and being open to discussing both positive and negative emotions. A respectful communicator provides non-judgmental support, seeks clarification when needed, and strives to understand the other person's perspective without imposing their own beliefs.

2. Empathy:

Empathy is the ability to understand and share the feelings of another person. It is one of the most crucial traits that nurtures healthy relationships. When we are empathetic, we can connect deeply with others, show genuine care, and validate their emotions. Empathy encourages trust and helps in the resolution of conflicts by fostering mutual understanding.

3. Trust:

Trust is the cornerstone of any successful relationship. It is built over time through consistent honesty, reliability, and transparent communication. Trust allows individuals to feel safe, secure, and comfortable in expressing their thoughts and emotions. By honoring commitments and maintaining confidentiality, we nurture trust and create a strong bond in our relationships.

4. Boundaries:

Healthy relationships require clearly defined boundaries that respect individual needs and values. Each person should have the space to express their opinions and establish their limits. Respecting boundaries ensures that both parties feel comfortable, and it helps in avoiding misunderstandings, conflicts, and resentment.

5. Equality and Mutual Respect:

In healthy relationships, individuals treat each other as equals, honoring their inherent worth and respecting their unique perspectives. Mutual respect acknowledges the similarities and differences between people, allowing for open dialogue and collaboration. It is crucial to foster an environment where every opinion is valued and heard without judgment.

6. Emotional Support:

Being emotionally supportive means offering encouragement, understanding, and comfort to our loved ones during challenging times. This trait involves being present, actively listening, and providing a shoulder to lean on. By showing empathy and compassion, we create a safe space for individuals to express their vulnerabilities and seek assistance without fear of judgment or rejection.

7. Healthy Conflict Resolution:

Conflict is a natural part of any relationship, but healthy conflict resolution is essential for nurturing respectful interactions. It involves addressing disagreements constructively, without resorting to aggression, blame, or personal attacks. By focusing on active listening, finding common ground, and compromising when necessary, conflicts can be transformed into opportunities for growth and understanding.

8. Appreciation and Gratitude:

Expressing gratitude and appreciation is a powerful way to foster healthy relationships. Genuine appreciation enhances the connection between individuals and reinforces positive behavior. By acknowledging and valuing one another's contributions, efforts, and qualities, we create a nurturing environment built on mutual admiration and respect.

9. Flexibility and Adaptability:

No relationship is static, and flexibility is key to navigating the ever-changing dynamics of interpersonal connections. Being open-minded and adaptable allows individuals to accommodate each other's evolving needs and aspirations. Embracing change and compromising when necessary promotes a harmonious relationship where growth and development are encouraged.

10. Patience:

Patience, a trait often undervalued but essential in healthy relationships, involves accepting and understanding that everyone has their own pace and setbacks. It entails giving others the time and space they need, offering support without rushing or imposing our own expectations. Patience allows relationships to flourish by fostering understanding, empathy, and acceptance.

Understanding and embodying the traits of respectful interactions can serve as a guiding compass to cultivate healthy relationships in our lives. By practicing effective communication, empathy, trust, setting boundaries, and demonstrating mutual respect, we create a foundation for harmonious connections. Offering emotional support, resolving conflicts constructively, expressing gratitude, and being flexible and patient contribute to long-lasting and fulfilling relationships.

Remember, healthy relationships require effort, commitment, and continuous growth. Embracing these traits in our interactions will not only improve the quality of our relationships but also contribute to our own personal development and overall happiness.

Guarding Against Future Manipulation: Staying Safe in New Connections

In today's interconnected world, forming new connections with people has become easier than ever before. Whether it's through social media platforms, online dating apps, or networking events, we have countless opportunities to meet new individuals and expand our social circles. While this seems like a positive development, it also exposes us to potential manipulation from unscrupulous individuals. Therefore, it is crucial to equip ourselves with the knowledge and tools to guard against future manipulation in these new connections. This chapter will explore various strategies and insights to ensure our safety and well-being when forming new connections.

Understanding Manipulation:

Manipulation is a psychological technique employed by individuals with ulterior motives. It involves exerting influence or control over someone's thoughts, feelings, or actions for personal gain. Manipulative individuals are often skilled at appearing friendly, trustworthy, and charismatic, making it difficult to identify their true intentions until it's too late. Therefore, recognizing the signs of manipulation is of utmost importance in staying safe in new connections.

1. Trust Your Intuition:

One of the primary weapons against manipulation is our intuition. Humans possess a remarkable ability to sense when something seems off, even if they cannot precisely articulate why. When forming new connections, it is essential to trust your gut instinct and intuition. If a person or situation feels uncomfortable or raises red flags, it's crucial to take a step back and evaluate the situation objectively.

2. Conduct Background Research:

In today's digital age, researching new acquaintances has become easier than ever before. Before investing time and energy into a new connection, take advantage of search engines and social media platforms to gather information about the individual. Look for any inconsistencies, suspicious activities, or red flags that may indicate potential manipulation. Online reviews and testimonials about the person or their past interactions can also provide valuable insights.

3. Set and Maintain Boundaries:

Manipulative individuals often exploit others' boundaries for personal gain. Therefore, it is essential to establish clear boundaries from the beginning of any new connection. Communicate your needs, expectations, and limits honestly and assertively. If someone repeatedly disrespects or pushes your boundaries, it may be a sign of manipulative behavior. In such cases, be prepared to reassess the connection and consider whether it aligns with your well-being.

4. Observe Patterns of Behavior:

Manipulative individuals often display consistent patterns of behavior that become more apparent over time. By observing how a person interacts with others, responds to challenges, or handles conflict, you can gain valuable insights into their true character. Look for signs of manipulation such as frequent lies, gaslighting, guilt-tripping, or excessive flattery. These tactics often indicate a manipulative agenda.

5. Seek Objective Opinions:

Our judgment can become clouded when we are emotionally involved in new connections. To stay safe, it is crucial to seek objective opinions from trusted friends or family members. Share your experiences and impressions of the new connection, and listen attentively to their feedback. Sometimes, those close to us can recognize red flags that we may have overlooked due to our emotional investment.

6. Practice Self-Care:

Manipulation can have severe psychological and emotional consequences. To guard against future manipulation, prioritize self-care and maintain your well-being. Engage in activities that bring you joy, connect with supportive friends, and seek professional help if needed. When you are in a good mental and emotional state, you are better equipped to identify and defend against manipulation.

7. Be Wary of Love Bombing:

Love bombing is a manipulation technique where an individual showers excessive affection, attention, and gifts on another person to quickly establish a deep emotional connection. While it may seem flattering on the surface, love bombing is often a red flag for manipulative behavior. Take time to evaluate the sincerity and authenticity of such gestures and ensure that the connection is built on mutual respect and trust.

8. Educate Yourself:

Knowledge is power when it comes to guarding against manipulation. Educate yourself on common tactics used by manipulative individuals, such as gaslighting, projection, or emotional blackmail. By familiarizing yourself with these techniques, you can identify them early on and take appropriate action to protect yourself.

Forming new connections can be an exciting and rewarding experience, but it also exposes us to potential manipulation. Equipping ourselves with the knowledge and strategies outlined in this chapter is essential to staying safe and maintaining our well-being. By trusting our intuition, setting boundaries, conducting thorough research, seeking objective opinions, and prioritizing self-care, we can guard against future manipulation and build connections that are genuine, supportive, and mutually beneficial.

Chapter 7: The Role of Society and Community in Gaslighting Awareness

Gaslighting, a form of psychological manipulation, has gained increasing attention in recent years. This insidious tactic involves the gradual eroding of an individual's confidence, perception, and sanity over time, ultimately leaving them doubting their own reality. Gaslighting occurs in various contexts, from personal relationships to workplace dynamics and even in broader societal structures. In this pivotal chapter, we will delve into the crucial role that society and community play in gaslighting awareness and prevention. By understanding and addressing the systemic nature of gaslighting, we can develop strategies to dismantle it and cultivate healthier, more compassionate communities.

Unveiling Societal Gaslighting Dynamics

Society holds significant power over shaping individuals' beliefs, values, and behaviors. It is within these societal structures that gaslighting flourishes, targeting marginalized groups, perpetuating oppression, and distorting collective narratives. For centuries, certain communities have been subject to gaslighting, often resulting in the internalization of harmful stereotypes, self-doubt, and diminished self-worth. Recognizing and dismantling these dynamics is crucial for achieving lasting change and fostering a more inclusive society.

Promoting Victim-Blaming Narratives: A Systemic Issue

One way society facilitates gaslighting is through the promotion of victim-blaming narratives. Victims of gaslighting are often made to question their own experiences and are discredited, while the gaslighter maintains influence and control. Society's tendency to blame victims reinforces harmful power imbalances and perpetuates gaslighting behaviors. Only by challenging victim-blaming narratives head-on can we create the necessary space for survivors to heal and flourish, while simultaneously holding gaslighters accountable for their actions.

Education as a Catalyst for Change

Education is a potent tool in combating gaslighting on a societal level. By incorporating comprehensive education on gaslighting and its effects into school curricula and community programs, we can raise awareness and equip individuals with the knowledge and skills to recognize and counteract gaslighting tactics. Such education should encompass teaching emotional intelligence, critical thinking, and healthy communication skills. Moreover, it is essential to highlight historical instances of gaslighting, such as the erasure and discrediting of marginalized communities, to foster empathy and promote lasting change.

Fostering Empathy and Active Listening

In cultivating gaslighting awareness, society must shift its focus from a superficial understanding of empathy to engaging in active listening and validation. This requires creating safe spaces where individuals can share their experiences without fear of judgment or gaslighting. By actively listening, learning from others' stories, and validating their feelings, we can empower survivors to reclaim their narratives and rebuild their self-confidence.

Challenging Systemic Power Structures

Gaslighting often derives its strength from systemic power structures that enable its perpetuation. Historical imbalances of power based on gender, race, socioeconomic status, and other factors contribute to the normalization of gaslighting behavior. Meaningful progress requires collective effort to challenge and dismantle these structures. By amplifying marginalized voices, promoting diversity and inclusion, and advocating for equal opportunities, society can disrupt the power dynamics that fuel gaslighting, ultimately fostering a more just and equitable world.

Community Support and Healing

Creating communities that prioritize support and healing is instrumental in combating gaslighting on a societal level. Through the establishment of support groups, counseling services, and community-led initiatives, survivors of gaslighting can find solace, validation, and the necessary tools for recovery. Communities must also work to hold gaslighters accountable for their actions, ensuring that they are educated about the repercussions of their behavior and given opportunities for growth and transformation.

Chapter 7 has explored the critical role of society and community in gaslighting awareness. From unveiling societal gaslighting dynamics to challenging victim-blaming narratives and fostering empathy, we have examined the potential strategies for dismantling gaslighting at a systemic level. Through education, empathy, and challenging systemic power structures, societal change becomes achievable.

As we move forward, it is crucial to remember that undoing centuries of gaslighting requires a collective effort. By prioritizing support, healing, and accountability within our communities, we can create a society that empowers individuals, celebrates diversity, and rejects gaslighting in all forms. Only then can we pave the way for an inclusive and compassionate future, free from the damaging effects of gaslighting.

Education as Enlightenment: Spreading Knowledge about Gaslighting

Education plays a vital role in empowering individuals and communities by cultivating critical thinking, promoting awareness, and fostering personal growth. In recent years, the term "gaslighting" has gained significant attention due to its manipulative nature and the potential harm it can cause to individuals' mental and emotional well-being. In this chapter, we will explore the concept of gaslighting, its various forms, and the importance of spreading knowledge about it through education. By shedding light on this insidious psychological tactic, we can empower individuals to recognize and navigate gaslighting situations with confidence.

Understanding Gaslighting

To comprehensively address the issue of gaslighting, it is essential to understand its origins and mechanisms. The term "gaslighting" finds its roots in the 1938 play, Gaslight, and its subsequent film adaptations. In this narrative, a husband manipulates his wife into believing she is going insane by purposefully altering their environment, leading her to question her own senses and perceptions.

Today, gaslighting refers to a psychological tactic employed by manipulative individuals to gain power and control over others. It involves systematically undermining someone's reality, often leading the victim to doubt their own sanity or question their memories. Gaslighters employ a range of tactics, including denying wrongdoing, trivializing the victim's emotions, and asserting their interpretation as the only valid one.

Forms of Gaslighting

Gaslighting manifests in various forms and contexts, affecting both personal relationships and broader societal dynamics. Recognizing these different manifestations is crucial for effectively addressing gaslighting and creating a more informed and empathetic society. Let's explore some common forms of gaslighting:

1. Personal Relationships: Gaslighting often occurs within intimate relationships, where one partner manipulates the other to feel powerless and dependent. This can involve constant criticism, belittlement, and undermining the victim's capabilities. Consequently, the victim's self-esteem erodes, making them easier to control.

2. Professional Environments: In the workplace, gaslighting can occur when employers or colleagues emotionally manipulate others, leading them to doubt their competence or contributions. Gaslighters may deny positive outcomes, assign blame unfairly, or even intentionally set colleagues up for failure, all with the aim of

controlling or discrediting them.

3. Cultural and Political Settings: Gaslighting is not limited to intimate relationships or professional environments. It can also occur on a broader scale when those in positions of power manipulate narratives, distort facts, or create disinformation campaigns to sow doubt, destabilize communities, or maintain their authority.

The Role of Education in Spreading Awareness

Education is central to combating gaslighting as it equips individuals with the critical thinking skills necessary to identify and address manipulative tactics effectively. By integrating education about gaslighting within school curricula, professional development programs, and community initiatives, we can create a more informed society capable of recognizing gaslighting and protecting themselves against its harmful effects. Here's how education can help:

1. Raising Awareness: Education serves as a powerful tool for raising awareness about gaslighting and its potential impact on individuals and communities. By incorporating lessons on recognizing and understanding gaslighting within various educational settings, we can empower individuals to identify manipulative behaviors early on.

2. Developing Critical Thinking Skills: Education should emphasize the development of critical thinking skills, fostering an environment

where individuals feel encouraged to question information presented to them. By nurturing students' ability to analyze sources critically and evaluate claims, we can build resilience against gaslighting attempts.

3. Encouraging Open Dialogue: Education provides a platform for open and honest discussions about gaslighting, creating safe spaces for sharing personal experiences and promoting empathy. By encouraging dialogue, we foster a sense of community and support among victims, making it easier for them to seek help and support one another.

Gaslighting, as a manipulative tactic, can have severe consequences on individuals' mental health, relationships, and overall well-being. However, by integrating education that raises awareness and cultivates critical thinking skills, we can empower individuals to recognize gaslighting and protect themselves against its harmful effects. Education serves as a catalyst for change, spreading knowledge and creating a society that is better equipped to challenge and dismantle gaslighting dynamics. Through continued efforts to educate ourselves and others, we can foster an enlightened society that champions empathy, authenticity, and the pursuit of truth.

Community Support Groups: Safe Spaces for Sharing and Healing

In today's fast-paced and often isolating world, the need for community support groups has become increasingly apparent. These groups offer a safe and supportive environment where individuals dealing with a range of challenges can come together to share their experiences, seek guidance, and find solace. Whether grappling with mental health issues, addiction, grief, or other difficulties, community support groups provide a lifeline for individuals seeking connection, understanding, and healing. This chapter explores the significance of these groups as safe spaces for sharing and healing, delving into their structure, benefits, and the lasting impact they have on individuals' lives.

Chapter 1: The Power of Community

Humans are inherently social beings, reliant on meaningful connections to thrive. However, in a society driven by technological advancement, genuine human connection has become increasingly elusive. This distance often engenders feelings of isolation, amplifying personal struggles and impeding healing. Community support groups counteract this trend by offering an empathetic community that fosters a sense of belonging. By recognizing that others also face similar challenges, individuals can find solace, validation, and compassionate understanding. The power of community support lies in its ability to harness collective strength, providing participants with a safe haven to confront their circumstances head-on.

Chapter 2: Enabling Shared Experiences

One of the most significant advantages of community support groups is the opportunity they present for shared experiences. By interacting with others who have gone through or are currently navigating similar challenges, individuals feel less alone in their struggles. Whether battling addiction or coping with the loss of a loved one, participants can exchange stories, lessons learned, and coping mechanisms. Sharing experiences not only enlightens individuals about different perspectives but also creates bonds of empathy and understanding within the group.

Chapter 3: Fostering Emotional Expression

The burden of emotional pain is lightened when shared among those who truly understand. Community support groups provide a space where individuals can openly express their emotions, free from judgment or shame. The act of verbalizing emotional struggles can be immensely cathartic, empowering participants to confront and process their feelings. The group becomes a sounding board, offering gentle guidance and encouragement while nurturing emotional resilience.

Chapter 4: A Network of Support

Community support groups play a pivotal role in establishing a network of support, which is crucial for individuals navigating difficult circumstances. These groups foster an environment where participants can lean on one another, offer insights, and lend a shoulder to cry on. Through shared experiences and mutual understanding, friendships are forged, and lasting support networks are created. Individuals feel safe knowing that they can rely on their community for encouragement, advice, and a listening ear during both good and challenging times.

Chapter 5: Empowering Individuals

When individuals face adversity, they may feel powerless or lost. Community support groups work to counteract these feelings by empowering individuals to take control of their lives. Through the shared experiences and collective wisdom of the group, participants gain new perspectives, coping skills, and strategies for healing. This empowerment leads to renewed confidence and a strengthened belief in their ability to overcome challenges.

Chapter 6: Breaking Stigmas

Community support groups serve as a platform for challenging and dismantling the stigmas associated with various issues like mental health, addiction, and grief. By openly discussing these topics in a non-judgmental space, participants help to dispel misconceptions and foster a greater understanding within their communities. As the group members embrace vulnerability and share their stories, they contribute to a society that is more empathetic and accepting.

Chapter 7: The Promise of Long-Term Healing

The tremendous impact of community support groups extends far beyond their members' participation. By fostering healing, resilience, and personal growth, these groups enable individuals to carry their newfound strength out into the world. Participants are not only inspired to continue their own healing journey but also become advocates who create positive change within their communities. The ripple effect of a single group's support can extend far, ultimately touching countless lives.

Legislative Measures: Protecting Victims at a Larger Scale

In recent years, there has been a growing acknowledgment of the need for legislative measures to protect victims of various forms of abuse and exploitation. Victims, both individuals and communities, have suffered silently for far too long, and it is imperative that our societies prioritize their safety and well-being. This chapter will delve into the legislative measures that can be adopted to ensure the protection of victims at a larger scale, focusing on key areas such as domestic violence, human trafficking, and child abuse.

I. Domestic Violence: Breaking the Cycle of Abuse

Domestic violence is a pervasive issue affecting millions of individuals worldwide. It encompasses physical, sexual, emotional, and economic abuse, perpetrated by a family member or intimate partner. To protect victims and prevent further abuse, robust legislative measures are essential.

1. Criminalization and Strict Penalties:
First and foremost, governments must criminalize domestic violence and enact strict penalties for offenders. This sends a clear message that such behavior will not be tolerated in society. Enhanced punishments for repeat offenders can act as a deterrent, saving

potential victims from further harm.

2. Restraining Orders:

The introduction of restraining orders can provide immediate relief and safety to victims. These legal orders restrict the abuser from approaching or contacting the victim, and violation of such orders should invite severe consequences. The effectiveness of restraining orders can be enhanced by implementing strict monitoring and enforcement mechanisms.

3. Establishing Shelters and Support Services:

Governments must invest in the establishment of shelters and support services specifically designed for victims of domestic violence. These safe havens can offer temporary accommodation, counseling, legal aid, and vocational training, enabling victims to rebuild their lives free from fear.

II. Combating Human Trafficking: Eradicating Modern Slavery

Human trafficking, a modern-day form of slavery, exploits vulnerable individuals for various purposes, including forced labor, sexual exploitation, and organ trafficking. To protect victims and eradicate this heinous crime, legislative measures must be implemented with a multi-pronged approach.

1. Comprehensive Legislation:

Governments should enact comprehensive legislation that criminalizes all aspects of human trafficking, from recruitment and transportation to harboring and exploitation. By defining clear offenses and prescribing severe penalties, legal frameworks can act as a deterrent and ensure justice for victims.

2. Protection of Victims:

Legislation should prioritize the protection of victims. This could include granting special visas or temporary residency status to trafficking survivors, ensuring they are not penalized for acts committed under duress. Governments must also establish specialized support services, offering comprehensive assistance, including medical care, counseling, and access to education and employment opportunities.

3. Collaboration and International Cooperation:

Effective legislative measures against human trafficking require international collaboration. Governments must join forces to strengthen border control measures, exchange information, and streamline legal processes for extradition and prosecution of perpetrators. Cooperation between law enforcement agencies, NGOs, and international organizations is crucial in tackling this global crime.

III. Combating Child Abuse: Ensuring a Safe Environment for Future Generations

Child abuse, encompassing physical, sexual, emotional, and neglectful mistreatment of minors, is a grave violation of their rights. Legislative measures play a pivotal role in preventing and addressing child abuse, ensuring the safety and well-being of our future generations.

1. Mandatory Reporting Laws:

Governments should enact mandatory reporting laws, requiring professionals who work with children, such as teachers, doctors, and social workers, to report suspected cases of abuse to the authorities. This legal obligation ensures early intervention and protection for victims.

2. Harsher Sentencing for Offenders:

Child abusers must face severe penalties to deter potential perpetrators. Sentencing guidelines should account for the heinous nature of these crimes, ensuring that punishment matches the severity of the offense. Additionally, repeat offenders should face increased penalties to safeguard vulnerable children from further harm.

3. Prevention and Awareness Programs:

Legislation should mandate the implementation of prevention and awareness programs in schools and communities. These initiatives can educate children, parents, and caretakers about child abuse, its signs, and preventive measures. By promoting awareness, these programs can empower communities to identify and report abuse, leading to early intervention.

The enforcement of robust legislative measures is fundamental to protecting victims of various forms of abuse and exploitation. Governments around the world must prioritize the enactment and implementation of comprehensive laws that criminalize perpetrators' actions, while providing victims with the necessary support, protection, and prevention services. By adopting legislative measures that address domestic violence, human trafficking, and child abuse, we can collectively work towards building a society that values the safety and well-being of all its members.

Promoting Empathy and Understanding: Shifting Cultural Narratives

In a rapidly globalizing world, the need for promoting empathy and understanding across cultures has become paramount. The interconnectedness of societies through technological advancements brings people from diverse cultural backgrounds closer together than ever before. Consequently, it becomes essential to shift cultural narratives to foster empathy and understanding among individuals. This chapter delves into the significance of promoting empathy, discusses the power of narratives in shaping cultural perspectives, and explores ways in which we can actively work towards reshaping these narratives.

Section 1: The Power of Empathy

Empathy is the ability to understand and share another person's feelings, experiences, and perspectives. It is a fundamental human trait that allows us to connect with others on a deeper level, transcending cultural barriers. By fostering empathy, we develop a sense of compassion and a willingness to appreciate cultural differences rather than perceiving them as threats.

Empathy plays a crucial role in counteracting harmful stereotypes, prejudices, and discrimination prevalent in society. It allows us to confront our biases and challenge the narratives that perpetuate division and misunderstanding. By promoting empathy, we create a more inclusive and harmonious world, where the richness of diverse cultures can thrive.

Section 2: The Power of Narratives

Narratives, whether in the form of stories, media, or historical accounts, shape our understanding of the world and our cultural perspectives. They can reinforce stereotypes and perpetuate biases or challenge them and encourage empathy. In this section, we explore the powerful influence of narratives on our cultural perception.

Cultural narratives are not fixed or static; they evolve over time and are subject to change. By understanding the impact of narratives, we can actively work towards reshaping them to promote empathy and understanding. This process involves reevaluating our own narratives and embracing alternative perspectives.

Section 3: Shifting Cultural Narratives

3.1 The Role of Education

Education plays a vital role in shifting cultural narratives to promote empathy and understanding. By integrating multicultural and inclusive curricula, education systems can expose students to diverse perspectives from an early age. This fosters empathy and helps break down cultural barriers. Moreover, educators can encourage critical thinking, empowering students to challenge existing narratives and develop their own empathetic understanding of different cultures.

3.2 Media Representation

Media is a powerful tool that shapes cultural narratives and contributes to our understanding of different cultures. By promoting accurate and positive representation of diverse cultures, media can dispel stereotypes and challenge biases. Media outlets and content creators have a responsibility to ensure inclusivity and provide platforms for marginalized voices to be heard. By doing so, they play a crucial role in shifting cultural narratives towards empathy and understanding.

3.3 Cultural Exchange Programs

Cultural exchange programs facilitate direct interaction between individuals from different cultural backgrounds. By experiencing another culture firsthand, we gain a deeper understanding and develop empathy through personal connections. Governments and organizations should invest in and promote such programs, fostering cultural exchange and bridging the empathy gap between diverse communities.

Section 4: The Individual's Perspective

Promoting empathy and understanding is not solely the responsibility of institutions and organizations. Each individual has a crucial role to play in actively reshaping cultural narratives.

4.1 Self-reflection and Acknowledging Bias

Individuals must engage in self-reflection and acknowledge their own biases. By confronting and challenging personal biases, we can start shifting our own narratives towards more empathetic perspectives. This internal transformation is a necessary precursor to fostering empathy and understanding at a societal level.

4.2 Cultural Immersion

Actively seeking opportunities to immerse oneself in different cultures is key to promoting empathy and understanding. This can involve traveling to different countries, engaging in local communities, or participating in cultural events. By embracing unfamiliar environments, individuals can gain firsthand experiences that challenge preconceived notions and nurture empathy.

4.3 Open-minded Dialogue

Engaging in open-minded dialogue with individuals from different cultural backgrounds encourages empathy and understanding. By listening to different perspectives without judgment, we create a safe space for cultural exchange and learning. Through active dialogue, we can challenge negative narratives and cultivate a more inclusive worldview.

Promoting empathy and understanding by shifting cultural narratives is a complex and ongoing process. It requires collective effort from individuals, institutions, and societies at large. By fostering empathy, acknowledging biases, and embracing diverse cultures, we can work towards a more united and harmonious world. This chapter serves as a starting point for understanding the significance of empathy and the power of narratives in shaping cultural perspectives. It is our collective responsibility to actively promote empathy and understanding, driving positive change in our increasingly interconnected global community.

Chapter 8: The Path Forward: Emerging Stronger from the Shadows

In the previous chapters of this book, we have explored the various aspects of life that often keep us hidden in the shadows. We have delved into deep-rooted fears, self-doubt, and limiting beliefs that hinder our growth and prevent us from fully embracing our true potential. Now, in Chapter 8: The Path Forward: Emerging Stronger from the Shadows, we will delve into the strategies and mindset needed to overcome these obstacles and step into the light.

Recognizing the Power Within

Before we can begin our journey towards emerging stronger from the shadows, we must first acknowledge the power that lies within us. Each of us possesses immense potential, waiting to be cultivated and unleashed upon the world. It is often our own self-critical thoughts and beliefs that keep us hidden away, doubting our abilities. But we must remember that we are capable of achieving greatness, and it is crucial to cultivate a positive mindset.

Reframing Fear

Fear has the uncanny ability to paralyze us and hold us back from pursuing our dreams. However, it is important to recognize that fear can also be a catalyst for growth. In this chapter, we will discuss the importance of reframing fear, shifting our perspective from seeing it as a hindrance to perceiving it as an opportunity for development.

Understanding Failure as a Stepping Stone

Too often, we allow our fear of failure to immobilize us, preventing us from taking risks and pursuing our goals. However, failure should not be seen as something to be avoided at all costs. Instead, we need to understand that failure is an essential component of growth. It is through our failures that we learn valuable lessons, gain resilience, and ultimately progress on our journeys towards success.

Building a Supportive Network

No one can truly emerge from the shadows alone. As we strive to step into the light, it is crucial to surround ourselves with a supportive network of individuals who believe in our dreams and aspirations. Whether it be friends, family, mentors, or like-minded individuals, their unwavering support can uplift us during moments of doubt and propel us forward.

Creating a Vision for the Future

To guide us on our journey of emerging stronger from the shadows, we must create a clear vision for our future. What are our ultimate aspirations? What steps do we need to take to achieve them? By developing a compelling vision, we provide ourselves with a roadmap, making it easier to navigate the challenges that lie ahead and ensure that we stay on track.

Setting Goals and Taking Action

A vision without action is merely a figment of our imagination. In this chapter, we will explore the importance of setting clear, achievable goals and taking consistent action towards their realization. By breaking our vision down into smaller, manageable targets, we lay the foundation for success and maintain momentum on our journey.

Embracing Self-Reflection and Growth

Personal growth and self-reflection are essential components of emerging stronger from the shadows. By taking the time to pause, evaluate, and learn from our experiences, we empower ourselves to make positive changes and confront the inner obstacles that hold us back. Embracing self-reflection allows us to continuously evolve and move closer towards our true potential.

Cultivating Resilience and Perseverance

No journey towards emerging stronger from the shadows is without its setbacks and challenges. However, it is through resilience and perseverance that we rise above adversity. In this chapter, we will discuss strategies for developing resilience, bouncing back from failure, and maintaining a steadfast determination in the face of obstacles.

Embodying Authenticity

Lastly, as we emerge stronger from the shadows, it is crucial to embrace our authentic selves. Society often pressures us to conform, but true fulfillment and success lie in embracing our uniqueness and staying true to our values. By honoring our individuality, we inspire others to do the same and create a ripple effect of positive change.

Chapter 8: The Path Forward: Emerging Stronger from the Shadows has explored the mindset and strategies needed to overcome the obstacles that keep us hidden away and embrace our true potential. By recognizing our power within, reframing fear, understanding failure, building a supportive network, creating a vision, setting goals, embracing self-reflection, cultivating resilience, and embodying authenticity, we can navigate our journey towards self-realization. Remember, emerging stronger from the shadows is a lifelong process, and each step forward is a victory in itself. Embrace the challenges, stay true to yourself, and never forget that you possess the strength to shine brightly in the world.

Resilience in Recovery: Drawing Strength from the Past

In the journey of recovery, individuals often face numerous challenges and obstacles that test their strength and determination. Navigating through these difficulties requires a unique quality known as resilience. Resilience can be defined as the ability to bounce back and thrive despite adversity. It is this resilience that allows us to grow, learn, and draw strength from our past experiences. In this chapter, we will explore the concept of resilience in recovery, its significance, and how individuals can harness their past to build a more robust foundation for the future.

Understanding Resilience:

Resilience is not an innate trait; rather, it is a skill that can be developed and nurtured. It is the force that enables individuals to confront life's challenges head-on, adapt to change, and emerge stronger and more self-assured. In recovery, it plays a critical role in helping individuals overcome setbacks, cope with triggers, and maintain their commitment to sobriety.

Resilience is not something that is acquired overnight, but rather a process that evolves over time. It is cultivated through a combination of personal experiences, supportive relationships, and the ability to reflect on past achievements and setbacks. In essence, resilience is an amalgamation of the lessons learned, the wisdom gained, and the courage to confront life's trials and tribulations with renewed strength.

Drawing Strength from the Past:

One of the most effective ways to develop resilience in recovery is by drawing strength from the past. Our past experiences, both positive and negative, shape who we are today and provide valuable lessons that can guide us through future challenges.

1. Reflection and Self-Awareness:

Taking the time to reflect on our past can help us gain a deeper understanding of ourselves and our recovery journey. By looking back, we can identify patterns, triggers, and vulnerabilities that may have led us to substance abuse. Reflecting on our successes and failures can illuminate the areas where we have grown and provide insights into our resilience. This self-awareness enables us to make informed choices, set realistic goals, and develop strategies to overcome obstacles.

2. Acknowledging and Celebrating Milestones:

Recovery is a journey marked by significant milestones, both big and small. Each milestone achieved represents a triumph over adversity and serves as a testament to our resilience. Celebrating these milestones and acknowledging our progress reinforces our ability to overcome challenges and motivates us to keep moving forward.

3. Learning from Setbacks:

Setbacks are an inevitable part of recovery. However, it is crucial to view them as learning opportunities rather than failures. When we encounter setbacks, we should ask ourselves what we can learn from the experience, how we can adapt our approach, and how we can strengthen our resilience in the face of similar obstacles in the future. By reframing setbacks as stepping stones rather than stumbling blocks, we can leverage them to fuel our resilience.

4. Gaining Inspiration from Role Models:

Throughout history, many individuals have faced adversity and triumphed over it. Drawing inspiration from these role models can instill hope and resilience in our own recovery journey. By studying the lives of those who have successfully overcome addiction or any other challenge, we can learn valuable strategies, techniques, and attitudes that can strengthen our resilience. Their stories remind us that resilience is not limited to a select few but is within the grasp of every individual committed to their recovery.

5. Building Supportive Relationships:

Being surrounded by a supportive network is instrumental in fostering resilience. Connecting with individuals who understand the challenges of recovery can provide a safe space to share experiences, seek guidance, and receive encouragement. Furthermore, emotional support from loved ones enables us to develop coping mechanisms, learn from their experiences, and draw strength from their unwavering support.

Advocacy and Empowerment: Using Your Experience for Change

In a society filled with countless challenges and inequalities, it is crucial that we harness the power of our experiences to bring about positive change. Advocacy and empowerment go hand in hand as they provide individuals with the tools to stand up for their rights, make their voices heard, and create lasting impact. This chapter aims to delve into the importance of advocacy and empowerment, while highlighting ways in which we can use our experiences to drive meaningful change in the world around us.

Understanding Advocacy

Advocacy is the act of supporting or speaking on behalf of a cause, issue, or group of individuals who face social, political, or economic barriers. It encompasses various strategies, including raising awareness, educating others, initiating policy changes, and promoting social justice. Advocacy plays a critical role in addressing systemic inequalities and ensuring that marginalized voices are heard.

Empowerment, on the other hand, focuses on enabling individuals to take control of their own lives, build their confidence, and develop the necessary skills to drive change. It aims to redress power imbalances and create an inclusive society that values diversity and equality. When combined, advocacy and empowerment become powerful tools that enable individuals to challenge social norms, fight injustice, and shape a better future.

The Importance of Personal Experience

Personal experiences serve as a catalyst for change. Our unique stories, struggles, and triumphs provide invaluable insights that can inform our advocacy efforts. By sharing our personal experiences, we can raise awareness, foster empathy, and mobilize others to take action. Moreover, our experiences lend credibility and authenticity to our advocacy work, making it more impactful and relatable.

When we harness the power of personal experience, we humanize the issues at hand, making them more tangible and compelling. For example, a person who has personally encountered housing insecurity can shed light on the challenges faced by those experiencing homelessness, putting a face and a story to a pervasive issue. By sharing their story, they can motivate others to get involved, effect change, and make a difference.

Sharing Your Story

One of the most powerful ways to advocate for change is through storytelling. Sharing our experiences in a compelling and authentic manner not only helps us heal and make sense of our journey but also invites others to connect with our narrative and empathize with our struggles. However, sharing one's story can often be daunting, as it requires vulnerability and the willingness to open up to others.

To effectively share your story, it is important to find a supportive space that values your voice. This could be through joining advocacy groups, participating in storytelling events, or utilizing digital platforms such as social media or blogs. It is crucial to remember that there is strength in numbers and that your story has the potential to inspire and initiate change.

Utilizing Social Media and Digital Platforms

In today's digitally connected world, social media and digital platforms offer powerful tools for advocacy and empowerment. Through these mediums, we can reach a wide audience, amplify our message, and mobilize individuals who share similar experiences or concerns. Social media enables us to create virtual communities, where our collective voices can be heard and our stories can create a ripple effect.

Platforms like Twitter, Facebook, and Instagram have increasingly become essential tools for grassroots advocacy movements. By sharing our experiences, insights, and informative content, we can educate, engage, and inspire others to take action. Social media also fosters dialogue and amplifies marginalized voices, ultimately pushing for systemic change.

Collaboration and Allyship

Advocacy and empowerment are not solitary endeavors. Creating lasting change often requires collaboration and allyship with like-minded individuals and organizations. By joining forces, we enhance our collective impact, pool resources, and create a more comprehensive and influential movement.

Collaboration goes beyond mere coordination; it requires active participation and a shared vision for change. By embracing allyship, we can harness the power of diverse perspectives, learn from one another, and broaden our understanding of the issues we aim to address. Together, we can create a network of change-makers who disrupt the status quo and advocate for a more just and equitable society.

Advocacy and empowerment are essential components of social change. By utilizing our experiences, sharing our stories, and engaging in collaborative efforts, we can challenge systemic inequalities and advocate for a better future. The power to effect change lies within each one of us – it is up to us to harness our experiences, amplify marginalized voices, and create a world where advocacy and empowerment are central tenets. Let us seize the opportunity to shape a more equitable and inclusive society, one where everyone has the opportunity to thrive.

Finding Peace in the Present: Mindfulness Techniques for Survivors

In the journey of healing and recovery, survivors often find themselves grappling with memories of the past, which can trigger feelings of anxiety, fear, and sadness. It is during these challenging moments that the practice of mindfulness becomes a powerful tool, allowing survivors to ground themselves in the present moment and find peace within. This chapter explores various mindfulness techniques specifically tailored for survivors, guiding them towards a state of inner calm and self-compassion.

Mindfulness and its Benefits for Survivors:

Before delving into the techniques, let's briefly discuss what mindfulness is and the benefits it offers to survivors. Mindfulness is the practice of purposely paying attention, without judgment, to the present moment. It involves anchoring oneself in the here and now, releasing attachment to past experiences or the anticipation of the future. Survivors who embrace mindfulness can experience several positive outcomes, including:

1. Reduced Anxiety: By focusing on the present, survivors can minimize the tendency to ruminate about past events or worry about future uncertainties, leading to a decrease in anxiety levels.

2. Enhanced Emotional Regulation: Mindfulness allows survivors to acknowledge their emotions without getting overwhelmed by them. By accepting their feelings, survivors can develop healthier coping mechanisms to regulate their emotions effectively.

3. Improved Self-Compassion: Survivors often carry guilt, shame, or self-blame, which hinders their healing process. Mindfulness nurtures self-compassion by cultivating an attitude of kindness and acceptance towards oneself, facilitating forgiveness and self-love.

Now, let's explore some mindfulness techniques specifically designed for survivors.

1. The Body Scan:

The body scan is a powerful technique to reconnect with the present moment and develop body awareness. Find a quiet, comfortable space and close your eyes. Start by bringing your attention to the top of your head and slowly scan down through your body, paying attention to any physical sensations, discomfort, or tension you might feel along the way. As you become aware of these sensations, allow yourself to release any tension or discomfort you encounter. By focusing on your body's sensations, you ground yourself in the present moment and create an opportunity for healing both physically and emotionally.

2. Five Senses Exercise:

This exercise engages all five senses and helps survivors connect with their immediate surroundings. Begin by taking a few deep breaths to center yourself. Then, identify:

- Five things you can see: Look around and notice five objects in your environment, observing their colors, shapes, and textures.
- Four things you can touch: Pay attention to the sensation of touch by identifying four objects that you can physically interact with and focusing on their tactile qualities.
- Three things you can hear: Listen carefully to your surroundings and notice three sounds that you can hear in that moment.
- Two things you can smell: Take a moment to identify two scents or smells in your surroundings. Breathe deeply and notice how they affect your senses.
- One thing you can taste: If possible, take a sip of water or something you have nearby. Pay close attention to the taste, texture, and temperature in your mouth.

By engaging all your senses, you shift your focus fully to the present, grounding yourself and finding solace through sensory experiences.

3. Loving-Kindness Meditation:

The practice of loving-kindness meditation cultivates a sense of unconditional love and compassion towards oneself and others. Start by finding a comfortable position and take a few deep breaths. In your mind, repeat the following phrases:

- May I be happy and free from suffering.
- May I be safe and protected from harm.
- May I be healthy and strong.
- May I live with ease and joy.

After a few minutes of focusing on yourself, redirect this loving-kindness towards someone you care about, then extend it towards neutral people and, finally, even to those who may have caused you harm. By practicing this meditation, survivors can gradually develop a sense of forgiveness, empathy, and interconnectedness.

Mindfulness techniques offer survivors the opportunity to find peace in the present moment, focusing on their well-being and self-compassion. Through practices like the body scan, the five senses exercise, and loving-kindness meditation, survivors can ground themselves, embrace their emotions, and release past burdens. As you embark on your mindfulness journey, remember that healing is a continuous process, and each step towards self-awareness and inner peace brings you closer to a healthier and happier future.

The Bright Future: A Life Beyond Gaslighting

Gaslighting, a form of psychological manipulation, has been present in our society for decades. It involves the distortion of reality, making victims question their own sanity, memory, and perception. It is a toxic tactic that erodes one's self-confidence, self-esteem, and overall well-being. In this chapter, we will explore the possibility of a brighter future, one that transcends the darkness of gaslighting, empowering individuals to reclaim their lives and embrace a new reality.

Understanding Gaslighting:

To move forward, it is crucial to fully comprehend the mechanics of gaslighting. Gaslighters use a range of tactics to manipulate their victims. They often deny their wrongdoing, distort the truth, trivialize their partner's experiences, or even blame the victim for their own actions. By doing so, they maintain control and power over others, leaving them feeling confused, helpless, and emotionally drained.

Recognizing the Signs:

The first step towards liberation lies in identifying gaslighting behaviors in our relationships, both personal and professional. It is essential to be aware of the red flags, such as constant questioning of one's judgment, frequent humiliation, undermining achievements, or minimizing emotions. By recognizing these signs, we can begin to break free from the grip of gaslighting and move towards a brighter future.

Reclaiming Our Power:

Moving beyond gaslighting requires reclaiming our power and trusting our instincts. It entails recognizing our own worth, questioning the narrative created by the gaslighter, and embracing our authentic selves. By acknowledging our strengths and rediscovering our passions, we can rebuild our self-confidence, thus establishing a solid foundation for a life free from gaslighting.

Finding Support:

No journey to healing can be undertaken alone. Seeking support is crucial in overcoming the effects of gaslighting. Support networks, such as friends, family, and therapy, play a vital role in validating our experiences and offering a safe space to heal. Sharing our stories with others who have experienced similar situations can be empowering, providing us with a sense of belonging and understanding.

Embracing Self-Care:

Self-care is a powerful tool in the journey towards a brighter future. Engaging in activities that bring us joy, cultivating healthy habits, and focusing on our mental and physical well-being are essential steps in reclaiming our lives. Practicing self-compassion and forgiveness allows us to let go of the self-doubt instilled by gaslighting, enabling us to move forward with renewed energy and positivity.

Setting Boundaries and Asserting Our Needs:

Developing healthy boundaries is crucial in establishing a life beyond gaslighting. It involves recognizing our limits, both emotional and physical, and asserting our needs. By clearly communicating our boundaries and expectations to others, we create a safe and supportive environment for ourselves, free from manipulation and control.

Rebuilding Trust:

Gaslighting shatters trust, leaving its victims skeptical of their own judgment and unsure of others' intentions. Rebuilding trust requires patience, self-reflection, and time. Developing trust in oneself is the first step, followed by gradually extending that trust to others. Surrounding ourselves with trustworthy individuals who respect our boundaries and support our growth is essential in this process.

Embracing a New Reality:

Creating a bright future beyond gaslighting necessitates embracing a new reality. It involves letting go of the pain, resentment, and self-doubt inflicted by the gaslighter. By reframing our experiences as valuable lessons rather than lingering wounds, we can cultivate a mindset focused on growth, resilience, and self-empowerment.

A Community of Empowered Survivors:

As we journey towards a life beyond gaslighting, it is important to remember that we are not alone. There are millions of survivors who share similar experiences, and together we can create a supportive community. Advocating for change, raising awareness, and sharing our stories can inspire and empower others, ensuring that no one else falls victim to the destructive cycle of gaslighting.

While gaslighting can leave deep scars, it is possible to emerge from its shadow and embrace a brighter future. By understanding the tactics of gaslighters, recognizing the signs, and taking proactive steps towards healing, we can rebuild our lives with strength, resilience, and self-love. Armed with knowledge and supported by a community of survivors, we have the power to break free from gaslighting and create a life filled with authenticity, joy, and personal growth. The journey to a life beyond gaslighting begins with self-belief and the unwavering determination to reclaim our power.

Chapter 9: Supporting Others through Gaslighting Recovery

In the journey of healing and recovery from gaslighting, it is crucial not only to focus on personal growth but also on supporting others who have fallen victim to this manipulative and destructive behavior. Gaslighting, a covert form of psychological abuse, can leave deep scars on the psyche of those who experience it. As a friend, family member, or confidante, your role in their healing process becomes paramount. This chapter will explore various ways to support and empower individuals as they navigate the treacherous path of gaslighting recovery.

Understanding Gaslighting:

To effectively support someone through their recovery journey, it is first essential to gain a clear understanding of gaslighting itself. Gaslighting is a manipulative technique where the perpetrator distorts the victim's perception of reality, making them doubt their own sanity, memory, and judgment. It involves deliberate psychological manipulation aimed at gaining power and control over the victim.

The Impact of Gaslighting:

Gaslighting can have severe and long-lasting effects on the victim's mental and emotional well-being. They may experience symptoms of anxiety, depression, self-doubt, and post-traumatic stress disorder. It is crucial to acknowledge the gravity of the impact gaslighting can have on a person's life.

Creating a Safe and Supportive Environment:

When supporting someone through gaslighting recovery, it is imperative to create a safe and supportive environment for them to heal. Allow them to express their thoughts, emotions, and experiences without judgment. Create an atmosphere where they feel heard and validated. By doing so, you provide them with a solid foundation on which to rebuild their self-esteem and trust.

Active Listening:

One of the most significant ways you can support someone on their journey of gaslighting recovery is through active listening. Actively listen to their experiences and emotions. Validate their feelings and assure them that their pain is real. Hearing them opens up space for them to process their thoughts and gain clarity on what they have been through.

Reinforcing Their Reality:

Gaslighting victims often struggle to distinguish between reality and the distorted version their abusers have fed them. As a supportive ally, you can help them re-establish their perception of reality. Offer tangible evidence or concrete examples to validate their experiences. By doing so, you help rebuild their self-trust, empowering them with the confidence to break free from the gaslighting's grip.

Rebuilding Self-Esteem:

Gaslighting relentlessly chips away at a person's self-esteem, leaving them questioning their worth and capabilities. Supporting someone in rebuilding their self-esteem is crucial for their recovery. Encourage them to engage in activities that reinforce their sense of self-worth and value. Remind them of their strengths, achievements, and qualities. By celebrating their successes, no matter how small, you aid in their journey of self-rediscovery.

Empowering Autonomy:

Gaslighting thrives by undermining a person's sense of autonomy and independence. To support someone through gaslighting recovery, help them reclaim their power and control over their own life. Encourage them to make decisions, both big and small, and support those choices without judgment. Rebuilding their confidence to trust their own judgment is a vital step in overcoming the effects of gaslighting.

Building a Supportive Network:

Being a supportive ally does not mean carrying the entire burden of their recovery alone. Encourage the gaslighting survivor to build a network of supportive individuals who can offer additional perspectives, advice, and comfort. Professional therapy or support groups specializing in gaslighting recovery can provide immense help. By expanding their support network, you equip the survivor with additional tools for their healing journey.

Setting Boundaries:

As a supporter, it is essential to establish and respect boundaries when helping someone recover from gaslighting. Recognize your own limitations and ensure you are not sacrificing your own well-being. Encourage the person to set their own boundaries as they regain control of their life. By respecting these boundaries, you demonstrate that their needs and autonomy are valued.

Education and Awareness:

Promoting education and awareness about gaslighting is crucial to prevent its occurrence and support survivors. Share resources, books, and articles on gaslighting and healthy relationships. By spreading knowledge, you equip others with the tools to identify gaslighting behaviors and provide support to those affected.

Supporting someone through gaslighting recovery is an honorable and compassionate endeavor. By actively listening, validating experiences, rebuilding self-esteem, and empowering autonomy, you can assist survivors on their journey towards healing. Remember that gaslighting recovery is a delicate and non-linear process, so your continued support and understanding are paramount. Together, we can create a society that stands against gaslighting and supports survivors on their path to reclaiming their lives.

Understanding the Supporter's Role: How to Be an Ally

In our journey towards progress and equality, we often come across individuals who require support and understanding. These individuals may belong to marginalized communities, face discrimination, or simply need help navigating life's challenges. This chapter delves into the crucial role of being an ally—an individual committed to empowering, advocating for, and standing with others. We will explore the foundations of allyship, recognize its significance, and delve into practical ways to become an effective and empathetic ally.

Section 1: Allyship Defined

The concept of allyship has emerged as a powerful tool to combat societal injustices. Allies actively work to dismantle oppressive systems and advocate for equity and inclusivity. To understand this role deeply, we must recognize the distinction between sympathy, empathy, and allyship:

1. Sympathy: Sympathy involves feeling sorry for someone's experiences or situation, often from a distance, without taking any active steps to address the root cause.

2. Empathy: Empathy, on the other hand, goes beyond sympathy. It involves understanding and sharing the feelings of others. Empathetic individuals are better equipped to understand the struggles faced by marginalized communities but may still lack the initiative to take action.

3. Allyship: Allyship moves beyond empathy. It requires individuals to actively educate themselves, stand up against injustice, and work collaboratively with marginalized communities to bring about positive change.

Section 2: The Significance of Allyship

2.1 Fostering Inclusivity and Equality:

Allyship is critical in creating an inclusive society that values and respects diversity. As allies, we have the opportunity to amplify marginalized voices, challenge harmful stereotypes, and ensure that everyone has an equal opportunity to thrive.

2.2 Sharing the Responsibility:

As members of a collective community, we should all shoulder the responsibility of advocating for equal rights and opportunities. Allies complement the efforts of marginalized communities by leveraging their privilege to address systemic inequalities.

2.3 Building Strong Relationships:

Allyship is not a one-time action; it is a commitment to supporting individuals and communities continuously. Through our actions, we can foster trust, build connections, and reinforce bonds that strengthen our society.

Section 3: Becoming an Ally

3.1 Educate Yourself:

To become an effective ally, education is essential. Take the time to educate yourself about the experiences faced by marginalized communities. Read books, attend workshops, and actively engage in conversations that broaden your perspective.

3.2 Listen and Learn:

Listening without judgment is a vital aspect of allyship. Create safe spaces where individuals can share their stories and experiences. Actively listen and learn from these narratives to better understand the issues at hand.

3.3 Amplify and Elevate Voices:

As an ally, you have the power to use your platform and privilege to amplify marginalized voices. Share their stories, achievements, and challenges. Use your influence to raise awareness and uplift the voices that have historically been silenced.

3.4 Challenge Your Own Biases:

It is crucial to acknowledge our own biases and work towards overcoming them. Reflect on your privileges and prejudices. Embrace discomfort and actively challenge your own biases to foster personal growth and transformation.

3.5 Speak Up Against Injustice:

Silence can be complicity. Allyship requires actively speaking up against discrimination, bigotry, and systemic injustices. Be prepared to engage in uncomfortable conversations, call out offensive behavior, and promote fairness when witnessing acts of injustice.

3.6 Offer Support and Take Action:

Support marginalized individuals by offering tangible assistance. This may include volunteering, donating, or becoming involved in grassroots community efforts. Advocate for policy changes that promote equality and social justice.

Section 4: Overcoming Challenges and Pitfalls

4.1 Accepting Criticism and Learning from Mistakes:

Allies may unintentionally make mistakes or misstep while

attempting to support others. It is essential to be open to feedback, accept criticism gracefully, and use those moments as opportunities for growth and improvement.

4.2 Centering Marginalized Voices:

As an ally, it is essential to center the experiences and perspectives of marginalized communities rather than imposing your own ideas. Act as a supportive accomplice, recognizing and following their leadership.

4.3 Embracing Intersectionality:

Recognize that individuals' experiences can be shaped not only by their identity but also by other intersecting factors, such as race, gender, sexuality, disability, and socio-economic status. Make an effort to acknowledge and understand these nuances.

Understanding the role of an ally is a crucial step towards building a fairer, more inclusive society. This chapter has highlighted the importance of allyship, provided practical ways to become an effective ally, and explored some of the challenges one may encounter on this journey. By committing to allyship, we can foster a world where everyone feels seen, valued, and supported. Let us stand together as allies to create a brighter future for all.

Effective Communication Strategies: Speaking with Empathy

In today's fast-paced world, effective communication has become increasingly important. It is not only about what we say but also how we say it and how well we connect with others on an emotional level. In this chapter, we will explore the art of speaking with empathy, understanding its significance, and learning effective strategies to enhance our communication skills.

Understanding Empathy

Empathy, often referred to as the ability to "put yourself in someone else's shoes," forms the cornerstone of effective communication. It is a powerful tool that allows us to connect with others on a deeper level, fostering understanding, trust, and respect. When we speak with empathy, we display genuine concern and compassion, ensuring that our message is not only heard but also understood.

Empathy involves actively listening to others, acknowledging their emotions, and providing support or comfort when needed. By empathizing with someone, we demonstrate that their feelings and experiences matter to us, creating a safe and inclusive space for open dialogue.

Recognizing the Importance of Empathetic Communication

Empathetic communication has a profound impact on various aspects of our lives, both personally and professionally. In personal relationships, empathy helps build strong bonds, resolves conflicts, and fosters a harmonious environment. It allows us to better understand our loved ones, sharing their joys and sorrows, and thus strengthening our connection with them.

In the professional realm, effective communication based on empathy is crucial for successful teamwork, leadership, and customer relations. Empathetic leaders inspire their teams, providing a supportive work environment that encourages collaboration and creativity. With customers, empathy helps us connect with their needs, building loyalty and trust, which are key to the success of any business.

Developing Empathy: Self-Awareness

Before we can effectively communicate with empathy, it is essential to develop a sense of self-awareness. Understanding our own thoughts, emotions, biases, and reactions is crucial in recognizing and minimizing any potential barriers to empathetic communication.

Taking the time to reflect on our own experiences and emotions allows us to gain insight into how others might be feeling and what they may need from us. While it may seem counterintuitive, focusing on ourselves first is an essential step in becoming more empathetic communicators.

Active Listening: The Foundation of Empathy

One of the fundamental components of effective communication with empathy is active listening. Active listening goes beyond just hearing the words being spoken. It involves giving our undivided attention to the speaker, observing non-verbal cues, and genuinely trying to understand their perspective.

To actively listen, start by maintaining eye contact and adopting an open body posture. By doing so, we show the speaker that we are fully present and ready to engage. It is important to resist the urge to interrupt or provide immediate solutions. Instead, let the speaker share their thoughts and feelings without any judgment or interference.

Additionally, paraphrasing and summarizing what the speaker has said can demonstrate our understanding and encourage them to elaborate further. Asking thoughtful, open-ended questions also encourages deeper conversation and allows the speaker to explain their emotions and experiences in more detail.

Empathy through Verbal Communication

While active listening lays the foundation for empathetic communication, how we respond verbally also plays a significant role. Using empathetic language and tone can convey our understanding, compassion, and support.

Firstly, it is crucial to use inclusive language that avoids making assumptions or generalizations about the speaker's feelings or experiences. Instead of saying, "I know how you feel," try asking open-ended questions such as, "How does this situation make you feel?" This enables the speaker to express their emotions in their own words, without feeling forced into a predefined response.

Secondly, using phrases such as "I understand" or "that must be challenging" conveys empathy and validates the other person's emotions. By acknowledging their feelings, we create a safe space for them to express themselves fully.

Lastly, it is essential to be mindful of our tone of voice. A warm, gentle tone can help create a supportive atmosphere, while a harsh or dismissive tone may discourage open communication.

Non-Verbal Communication and Empathy

Non-verbal communication is a powerful tool in expressing empathy. Our body language, facial expressions, and gestures can often convey more meaning than our words alone. Being aware of our non-verbal cues can help us communicate empathy effectively.

Maintaining eye contact and nodding our heads can show the speaker that we are actively engaged and interested in what they have to say. It is important to avoid crossing our arms or displaying defensive gestures, as these can create barriers to open conversation.

Facial expressions also play a vital role in empathetic communication. A genuine smile, a concerned look, or a compassionate expression can convey empathy and make the speaker feel understood.

Additionally, our proximity to the speaker can impact empathetic communication. Being physically closer can create a sense of intimacy and connection. However, it is crucial to respect personal boundaries and make sure the speaker is comfortable with our proximity.

Cultural Considerations and Empathetic Communication

When speaking with empathy, it is essential to consider cultural differences and norms, as they can greatly influence communication styles and expectations. Different cultures may have varying interpretations of empathy, and what is considered empathetic in one culture may not be in another.

Recognizing and respecting these cultural nuances allows us to adapt our communication strategies to effectively connect with individuals from diverse backgrounds. For example, more indirect communication might be appreciated in some cultures, while others may value direct and straightforward expressions of empathy.

It is important to approach cross-cultural communication with an open mind and a willingness to learn about different perspectives. By asking respectful questions and being attentive to cultural cues, we can foster empathy and understanding across cultural boundaries.

Practicing Empathetic Communication

Although it may seem daunting at first, practicing empathetic communication is achievable by following a few key strategies:

1. Patience and Time: Allow sufficient time for meaningful conversations. Rushing or being impatient can hinder the development of empathy and understanding.

2. Empathy as a Habit: Make empathy a part of your daily interactions. Practice empathy not only in significant conversations but also in everyday exchanges, such as with colleagues, friends, or even strangers.

3. Stepping Outside Your Comfort Zone: Challenge yourself to engage with diverse perspectives and experiences. This can help broaden your understanding and increase your capacity for empathy.

4. Reflect and Learn: Regularly reflect on your communication experiences. Identify areas where you struggled to display empathy and find ways to improve.

With consistent practice and a genuine desire to connect with others, speaking with empathy can become a natural and empowering aspect of our communication style.

In this chapter, we explored the significance of empathetic communication and learned effective strategies to enhance this crucial skill. Empathy is the bridge that connects us to others, allowing us to understand their emotions and experiences on a deep level. By actively listening, choosing empathetic language, and being mindful of non-verbal cues, we can create meaningful connections and foster understanding.

Remember, empathy is an ongoing practice. By cultivating self-awareness, actively listening, and being open to different perspectives, we can continue to improve our empathetic communication skills and build stronger, more empathetic relationships in every aspect of our lives.

Providing a Safe Space: Emotional Support and Encouragement

In the journey of life, we all encounter challenging times that make us vulnerable and in need of emotional support and encouragement. Whether it is a difficult breakup, the loss of a loved one, or battling mental health issues, having a safe space to share our thoughts and feelings can make a world of difference. This chapter delves into the importance of providing emotional support and encouragement, exploring various strategies and techniques to create a safe haven for those who need it most.

Understanding Emotional Support:

Emotional support refers to the provision of empathy, understanding, and compassion to individuals experiencing emotional distress or hardship. It involves creating an environment where individuals feel comfortable expressing their emotions without judgment or fear of rejection. Offering emotional support can transcend mere friendship, for it requires actively listening, validating feelings, and providing a comforting presence.

The Power of Listening:

One of the most fundamental aspects of providing emotional support is the ability to truly listen. Listening is not merely hearing words; it involves being fully present and attentive to the speaker, acknowledging their emotions and experiences. It is crucial to create a space that encourages open communication, allowing individuals to freely express their thoughts and feelings.

Active listening techniques such as maintaining eye contact, nodding empathetically, and asking open-ended questions can foster a deeper connection. Additionally, practicing reflective listening by paraphrasing what the speaker has shared helps affirm that their feelings have been heard and understood. By engaging in active listening, we demonstrate our genuine concern and willingness to support those in need.

Non-judgmental Attitude:

Creating a safe space for emotional support requires adopting a non-judgmental attitude. Judgment often stems from personal biases, preconceived notions, or a lack of understanding. However, dismissing or belittling someone's emotions can worsen their distress and create a barrier to seeking support.

To foster an environment of acceptance, it is essential to suspend judgment and approach others with empathy and compassion. Remember that everyone experiences emotions differently, and what may seem insignificant to one person can be incredibly distressing to another. A non-judgmental attitude acknowledges and respects the unique experiences and feelings of each individual.

Validation and Empathy:

Validation plays a pivotal role in emotional support, providing individuals with a sense of understanding and acceptance. Validating someone's emotions means recognizing and acknowledging their feelings as both real and significant. By doing so, we communicate that their experiences matter and are worthy of attention.

Empathy, on the other hand, involves putting ourselves in someone else's shoes, trying to understand their emotions from their perspective. Instead of providing unsolicited advice or attempting to solve the problem, empathy allows us to connect at a deeper level and relate to their feelings genuinely.

When offering emotional support, validating and expressing empathy can be as simple as saying, "I understand how that must feel," or "It sounds like you're going through a difficult time." These small gestures can make a significant impact, reassuring individuals that their emotions are valid and that they are not alone in their struggles.

Encouragement and Motivation:

Emotional support is not limited to listening and validating; it also involves encouraging and motivating individuals to overcome challenges. Providing optimism, reassurance, and hope can inspire individuals to persevere and find the strength to move forward.

To offer effective encouragement, it is essential to focus on the individual's strengths and resilience. Remind them of past achievements and their ability to overcome obstacles. Encourage self-reflection and self-compassion, helping them recognize their worth and potential.

Active encouragement can take various forms, such as praising efforts, celebrating progress, or offering constructive feedback when needed. Tailoring our approach to each person's unique needs and preferences can amplify the impact of our encouragement.

Creating a Safe Physical Environment:

In addition to the emotional atmosphere, creating a safe physical environment is equally crucial in ensuring emotional support. A comfortable and welcoming space can help individuals feel secure and at ease, further facilitating their emotional expression.

Consider factors such as lighting, privacy, and noise level when creating a safe physical space. Ensuring confidentiality and respecting boundaries are also essential to build trust. By providing a safe physical environment, we convey that emotional support is not only verbal but also extends to the physical environment.

Support for Emotional Well-being:

Apart from individual support, communities, organizations, and institutions must foster an environment that values emotional well-being. This includes implementing policies and resources to address mental health needs, promoting open conversations about emotions, and destigmatizing seeking professional help when necessary.

By prioritizing emotional well-being, we can create a society where individuals feel empowered to seek support and share their struggles. Recognizing emotional support as a fundamental human need fosters a culture of compassion, understanding, and resilience.

Providing a safe space for emotional support and encouragement is a powerful way to uplift and empower individuals during difficult times. Through active listening, non-judgmental attitudes, validation, and empathy, we can create an environment where individuals feel understood, accepted, and motivated to overcome their challenges.

Remember, emotional support extends beyond offering a listening ear; it necessitates creating a safe physical space and fostering an overall culture of emotional well-being. By incorporating these practices into our lives, we can make a significant difference in the lives of those around us, supporting them through their struggles, and enabling them to find healing and strength.

Collaborating with Professionals: Working with Therapists and Counselors

In today's fast-paced and demanding world, many individuals find themselves struggling with various emotional and mental health issues. In such times, seeking professional assistance from therapists and counselors has become increasingly important. These dedicated professionals possess the knowledge, skills, and experience to guide individuals towards healing and personal growth. However, collaborating effectively with therapists and counselors is vital for maximizing the benefits of therapy. This chapter explores the essential aspects of working with these professionals to ensure a productive and fruitful therapeutic journey.

Understanding the Role of Therapists and Counselors

To develop effective collaboration with therapists and counselors, it is crucial to understand their roles and the services they provide. While the terms "therapist" and "counselor" are often used interchangeably, there are some distinctions to consider. Therapists generally have advanced degrees, such as Ph.D. or Psy.D., and provide treatment for complex mental health conditions. They may include psychologists, psychiatrists, or licensed clinical social workers.

On the other hand, counselors might have a master's degree or a counseling-specific certification. Their focus is usually on providing guidance and support to individuals dealing with common life challenges and transitions. These may include marriage and family counselors, career counselors, or substance abuse counselors. Understanding these differences will help individuals make informed decisions when choosing a professional who aligns with their specific needs.

Building Trust and Rapport

A cornerstone of effective collaboration with therapists and counselors is building a trusting and supportive relationship. Initially, it may feel daunting to open up to a stranger about personal struggles. However, it is important to remember that therapists and counselors are bound by professional ethics and confidentiality, ensuring that client information remains private and secure.

To establish trust, it is essential to find a therapist or counselor with whom you feel comfortable and compatible. Look for professionals who demonstrate empathy, active listening skills, and genuine interest in your well-being. Asking for referrals from trusted friends or family members or conducting thorough research online can help in finding a professional who suits your individual preferences and needs.

Setting Clear Goals and Expectations

Having clear goals and expectations is crucial for effective collaboration with therapists and counselors. Before commencing therapy, take some time to reflect on what you hope to achieve through the therapeutic process. As an active participant, you can work with your therapist or counselor to set achievable and realistic goals tailored to your unique circumstances.

Communicating these goals and expectations with your therapist is vital. This open dialogue will encourage a shared understanding of what you wish to accomplish and how therapy or counseling sessions should be structured. Additionally, discussing the duration of therapy, the frequency of sessions, and the theoretical approach your therapist utilizes will provide a framework for your collaborative journey.

Active Engagement and Participation

Collaboration with therapists and counselors requires active engagement and participation from both parties. While therapists possess the expertise, individuals seeking therapy are the experts on themselves. Therefore, it is crucial to actively engage in the therapeutic process, being open and honest about thoughts, feelings, and experiences. Avoid withholding information, as this may hinder progress towards healing and growth.

During therapy or counseling sessions, it is important to actively communicate your thoughts and feelings, even if they seem challenging or uncomfortable to address. Remember that your therapist or counselor is a neutral and objective guide on your journey, and their insights can prove invaluable in helping you navigate through difficult emotions and unresolved issues.

Embracing the Process

Therapy and counseling involve a diverse range of evidence-based techniques and approaches. Embracing the process and remaining open to trying new strategies can enhance the therapeutic experience. Recognize that therapeutic progress may not always be linear. There may be ups and downs throughout the journey, and setbacks are a natural part of the healing process.

Working with a therapist or counselor requires a commitment to personal growth and a willingness to challenge deeply ingrained patterns and beliefs. Engaging in therapeutic homework assignments, practicing new coping skills outside of therapy, and reflecting on sessions will contribute to the overall effectiveness of the therapy.

Collaborating Outside the Therapy Room

Effective collaboration extends beyond the confines of therapy or counseling sessions. Engaging in self-care practices and implementing the strategies learned in therapy into daily life allows for continuous growth and development. It is important to take responsibility for your well-being and make efforts to incorporate newfound insights and coping mechanisms into everyday routines.

Additionally, including loved ones in the therapeutic journey can foster supportive relationships and aid in the overall healing process. Sharing insights gained from therapy sessions with trusted individuals can help deepen understanding and build a strong support network.

Collaborating with therapists and counselors is a valuable resource on the path to emotional well-being and personal growth. By establishing trust, setting clear goals, actively engaging in the therapeutic process, embracing the journey, and incorporating therapy into daily life, individuals can optimize the benefits of therapy. Remember, therapy is a partnership, and effective collaboration with professionals ensures a transformative and empowering experience.

Chapter 10: Reflection and Continuous Growth: Life after Gaslighting

In the previous chapters of this book, we have explored the insidious nature of gaslighting and its profound impact on the lives of its victims. We have delved into the tactics used by gaslighters and examined the emotional turmoil experienced by those who have fallen prey to this manipulative behavior. Now, it is time to embark on a journey of healing, reflection, and continuous growth that follows life after gaslighting.

The Aftermath

When the fog of gaslighting lifts, and the truth begins to unravel, victims often find themselves grappling with a multitude of emotions. The revelation that their reality has been distorted and their experiences invalidated can leave them feeling lost, confused, and unsure of who they are. The aftermath of gaslighting can be a disorienting and arduous process as survivors attempt to reclaim their sense of self and rediscover their own truth.

Reflection and Self-Awareness

One of the first steps towards healing from gaslighting involves embarking on a journey of self-reflection and introspection. It is imperative for survivors to reacquaint themselves with their own thoughts, feelings, and desires. This process often involves unraveling the web of lies that gaslighters spun and reconnecting with their authentic selves.

Rebuilding their self-esteem and self-worth may also become a focal point for survivors. Gaslighting can systematically erode one's confidence and self-belief. Engaging in activities that promote self-care and self-compassion can help rebuild and strengthen one's sense of self-worth. Additionally, seeking therapy or support groups can provide a safe space for survivors to process their experiences and work towards regaining their self-esteem.

Understanding the Impact

One of the more profound challenges in life after gaslighting is coming to terms with the lasting impact it has had on one's mental and emotional well-being. Gaslighting can result in long-lasting effects such as anxiety, depression, and post-traumatic stress disorder (PTSD). Survivors must acknowledge these impacts and understand that seeking professional help is not a sign of weakness but rather a courageous step towards healing.

In order to navigate life after gaslighting, survivors often find it beneficial to educate themselves about the psychological mechanisms behind gaslighting and its lasting effects. This knowledge equips survivors with the tools needed to challenge the self-doubt and second-guessing that may still persist even after the gaslighter is no longer present. It allows them to distinguish between facts and fiction, empowering them to reclaim their autonomy and establish healthier boundaries.

Rebuilding Relationships

Gaslighting can isolate survivors from their support networks, as perpetrators often manipulate the victim's perception of reality, making them doubt the intentions and trustworthiness of others. Rebuilding relationships with friends, family, and loved ones can be a crucial part of the healing process.

Survivors may need to extend themselves grace during this process, as rebuilding trust can be a slow and delicate endeavor. Honest and open communication is key, allowing survivors to express their experiences and emotions effectively while providing loved ones an opportunity to learn and grow from their past shortcomings.

Embracing Growth and Resilience

While the impact of gaslighting is undoubtedly profound, it is important for survivors to recognize that their journey does not end with healing. Life after gaslighting can serve as an opportunity for continuous growth and the cultivation of resilience.

Survivors often realize just how resilient they truly are. Having endured the emotional manipulation and survived, they emerge with a newfound strength and resilience that can be harnessed to navigate future challenges. They leverage their experiences to become more attuned to their own emotions, boundaries, and needs, enabling them to live a more authentic and fulfilling life.

Forgiveness and Closure

The process of forgiving the gaslighter can be complex, and it is important to remember that forgiveness is a personal journey that varies for each survivor. Forgiveness does not mean excusing or forgetting the gaslighter's actions. Instead, it allows the survivor to release the burden of anger, resentment, and bitterness that may hinder their own healing.

Closure, on the other hand, may come in various forms for different survivors. It may involve confronting the gaslighter, writing a letter expressing the unspoken words, or finding solace in understanding that they are no longer entangled in the web of deception. Closure empowers survivors to put the past behind them and fully embrace the possibilities that lie ahead.

Chapter 10, Reflection and Continuous Growth: Life after Gaslighting, offers survivors a roadmap to healing, self-reflection, and personal growth. It provides guidance on reestablishing their sense of self, understanding the impact of gaslighting, rebuilding relationships, embracing growth and resilience, and finding forgiveness and closure. While the journey may be difficult, survivors emerge from the chaos of gaslighting with a newfound strength and a renewed sense of self, ready to embrace a life filled with authenticity, contentment, and continuous growth.

Reflecting on the Journey: Lessons Learned and Growth Achieved

As we embark on the final leg of our journey, it's only fitting that we take a moment to pause, reflect, and ponder the invaluable lessons we have learned along the way. Life is a series of experiences, each contributing to our growth and shaping us into the individuals we become. The challenges we conquer, the triumphs we celebrate, and the mistakes we make—every twist and turn, both joyful and painful, plays a role in our personal development.

In this chapter, we will delve into some of the profound lessons that life has taught us, and explore the growth we have achieved through these experiences. So, let us take a moment to explore the tapestry of wisdom woven from the threads of our journey, and discover the invaluable insights hidden within.

1. Embracing Change:

One of the most crucial lessons we have learned is the significance of embracing change. Change is the only constant in life, and resisting it only hinders our growth. As we moved through the varying landscapes of our lives, we discovered that change often leads us to unexpected and remarkable opportunities. It is in those moments of discomfort and uncertainty that we have the chance to rise, adapt,

and soar to new heights. By embracing change, we have learned to
trust in the mysterious ways life unfolds.

2. Courage in the Face of Fear:

As human beings, fear is an emotion that lurks within us all.
However, we have emerged stronger by confronting our fears head-
on. Whether it was stepping into the unknown, tackling a daunting
challenge, or embracing vulnerability, we have discovered that fear
is nothing more than an illusion holding us back. We have learned
that courage is not the absence of fear, but rather the ability to act in
the face of it. Through our collective experiences, we have witnessed
the immense power that lies within us when we push past our fears.

3. Resilience: Bouncing Back From Adversity:

Life is never all smooth sailing, no matter how favorable the wind
may seem at times. The true measure of our character lies in our
ability to bounce back from adversity. We have encountered
setbacks, faced failures, and experienced heartbreak, but through it
all, we have developed the strength to rise and thrive once more. Our
journey has taught us that resilience is not merely a skill; it is a
mindset—a choice we make in the face of every setback, refusing to
be defined by our circumstances.

4. The Power of Relationships:

Human connections are the threads that weave the fabric of our lives. From family to friends to mentors, our relationships have played a vital role in our growth. They have provided support when we felt weak, offered guidance when we felt lost, and celebrated our victories alongside us. Our journey has demonstrated that investing time and energy in fostering meaningful connections not only brings joy but also propels us forward on the path to self-discovery.

5. The Art of Mindfulness:

In a fast-paced world filled with distractions, we have come to understand the importance of mindfulness. Mindfulness is the practice of being fully present in the moment, savoring each experience with a heightened appreciation. Through our journey, we have realized that it is in these quiet moments of reflection that we gain profound insights about ourselves and the world around us. Mindfulness has taught us to pause, breathe, and truly appreciate the journey, rather than merely rushing toward our destinations.

6. Self-Reflection: The Mirror of Growth:

Although the external world has provided us with numerous lessons, the most profound growth often comes from within. By engaging in self-reflection, we have gained a deeper understanding of our own strengths, weaknesses, and values. Self-reflection allows us to analyze our actions, motivations, and beliefs, enabling personal growth on a profound level. Through the practice of self-reflection, we have come to realize that true transformation begins when we turn our gaze inward and courageously confront our own shadows.

7. The Beauty of Patience:

In an era of instant gratification, patience has become a rare virtue. Yet our journey has taught us the immeasurable significance of cultivating patience. Many of the achievements and breakthroughs we have experienced required time and perseverance. We have learned to appreciate the beauty in the process, trusting that the seeds we sow will blossom in due course. Patience has gifted us with the ability to savor the journey rather than fixate solely on the destination.

As we reflect upon the voyage we have traveled, we are humbled by the lessons we have learned and the growth we have achieved. Life has been our greatest teacher, challenging us, molding us, and illuminating our path forward. Each step we have taken has brought us closer to self-awareness, compassion, and resilience.

In closing this chapter, we invite you to pause and reflect on your own journey. What lessons have life bestowed upon you, and how have you grown as a result? Cherish the wisdom gained from your experiences, as they are the stepping stones to a future filled with limitless possibilities. And remember, the journey is never truly complete—for each new day brings fresh lessons, new growth, and infinite opportunities for self-discovery.

Continued Personal Development: Strategies for Ongoing Healing

In our journey of personal growth and healing, it is essential to recognize that healing is not an event but a lifelong process. While significant progress can be made through various therapies and interventions, it is imperative to continue working on our growth and well-being consistently. In this chapter, we will explore strategies for ongoing healing that can support our continued personal development. These strategies are designed to inspire self-reflection, encourage growth, and maintain our emotional well-being over time.

1. Cultivating Self-Awareness:

One fundamental aspect of continued personal development is self-awareness. Developing self-awareness allows us to gain insight into our emotions, thoughts, behaviors, and patterns. It is through this awareness that we can identify areas that require attention, healing, and growth. Engaging in practices like journaling, mindfulness, and introspection fosters self-awareness, leading to increased personal understanding and exploration.

2. Embracing Emotional Intelligence:

Emotional intelligence refers to the ability to recognize, understand, and manage our emotions effectively. This skill enables us to develop healthy coping strategies, strengthen relationships, and make better decisions. By incorporating emotional intelligence into our lives, we become more adept at recognizing emotional triggers, processing our feelings, and responding to challenging situations with empathy and resilience.

3. Practicing Mindfulness:

Mindfulness brings our attention to the present moment, allowing us to experience life fully. By practicing mindfulness, we can cultivate a non-judgmental awareness of our thoughts, emotions, and bodily sensations. This awareness helps us detach from negative thought patterns and cultivate a sense of calm and balance. Mindfulness practices such as meditation, deep breathing exercises, or engaging in activities with focused attention enable us to stay present, reducing stress, and promoting overall well-being.

4. Prioritizing Self-Care:

Engaging in self-care activities is crucial for ongoing healing. Self-care involves carving out time for activities that nourish our physical, emotional, and mental well-being. This includes getting enough sleep, maintaining a nutritious diet, engaging in regular exercise, and pursuing hobbies or activities that bring us joy. By prioritizing self-care, we can replenish our energy, reduce stress, and nurture a sense of balance in our lives.

5. Building Resilience:

Resilience is the ability to adapt and bounce back from adversity. Continuously developing resilience is vital for ongoing healing as it equips us with the tools to navigate life's challenges. Developing resilience involves adopting a growth mindset, learning from setbacks, seeking support from others, and practicing self-compassion. By building resilience, we can face life's inevitable hurdles with greater strength and determination.

6. Seeking Support:

Healing and personal development are not solo endeavors. It is essential to seek support in our ongoing journey. This support can come from various sources, such as friends, family, mentors, coaches, or therapists. Sharing our experiences, vulnerabilities, and goals with trusted individuals provides us with invaluable perspectives and guidance. Additionally, engaging in support groups or professional therapy can offer specialized expertise and a nurturing environment for growth and healing.

7. Practicing Gratitude and Positive Thinking:

Cultivating gratitude and fostering positive thinking contribute significantly to our ongoing healing. By intentionally focusing on the positive aspects of our lives and expressing gratitude, we shift our mindset towards abundance and appreciation. Developing a daily gratitude practice can enhance our mood, increase resilience, and improve overall well-being. Additionally, practicing positive self-talk and reframing negative thoughts can empower us to overcome challenges and maintain a positive outlook on life.

8. Setting Meaningful Goals:

Having clear and meaningful goals provides us with a sense of purpose and direction in our ongoing healing journey. Goals can be both short-term and long-term, and they should align with our values and aspirations. By setting realistic and achievable goals, we can motivate ourselves to take consistent action towards personal growth and healing. Regularly reviewing and adjusting these goals ensures that we stay on track and continue moving forward in our journey.

9. Embracing Lifelong Learning:

Personal development is a continuous process that thrives on learning and growth. Embrace the mindset of a lifelong learner by seeking out new knowledge, exploring new interests, and challenging yourself intellectually. This can be accomplished through reading books, attending seminars, taking courses, or engaging in discussions with individuals who share similar interests. By embracing lifelong learning, we open ourselves to new perspectives, broaden our horizons, and deepen our understanding of ourselves and the world around us.

In this chapter, we explored strategies for ongoing healing and personal development. We recognized the importance of self-awareness, emotional intelligence, mindfulness, and self-care in maintaining our well-being. We discussed the significance of resilience, seeking support, and practicing gratitude and positive thinking. Additionally, we emphasized the value of setting meaningful goals and embracing lifelong learning in our continuous journey of growth. By incorporating these strategies into our lives, we can lay a solid foundation for ongoing healing, personal growth, and the pursuit of meaningful and fulfilling lives.

Connection and Community Engagement: Building Positive Relationships

In our fast-paced and technology-driven world, creating and cultivating meaningful connections has become more important than ever. We are often caught up in our busy schedules, constantly glued to our digital devices, and inadvertently neglecting the significance of personal relationships. However, humans are social creatures by nature, and establishing a strong network of connections within our community has numerous benefits for our mental, emotional, and physical well-being. In this chapter, we will explore the art of building positive relationships, fostering community engagement, and embracing the endless possibilities that come with genuine human connections.

Understanding the Power of Connection:

At its core, connection serves as the glue that binds individuals, groups, and societies together. In the age of social media, it is easy to fall into the trap of superficial interactions, focusing more on the quantity rather than the quality of our relationships. True connection goes far beyond the number of followers we have on Instagram or the amount of likes we receive on Facebook. It entails empathy, understanding, and an authentic desire to truly know and support one another.

Building strong connections begins with self-awareness and a willingness to be vulnerable. By being open and sharing our own experiences, dreams, and challenges, we create an environment that encourages others to do the same. This reciprocal sharing fosters trust, deepens bonds, and ultimately brings about long-lasting relationships.

Nurturing Healthy Relationships:

To cultivate and maintain healthy relationships, it is essential to invest time and energy in the people around us. This involves active listening, showing empathy, and being present during interactions. By truly hearing and understanding someone, we demonstrate that their thoughts and feelings matter, thus creating a foundation for a positive connection.

Additionally, genuine curiosity and a willingness to learn from others are key ingredients for building positive relationships. People have unique perspectives, experiences, and knowledge to share. Approaching conversations with a genuine desire to learn and grow not only enriches our own lives but also strengthens the connection we have with others.

Breaking Down Barriers of Community Engagement:
Community engagement serves as a gateway to meaningful connections and is a vital aspect of building a positive society. Unfortunately, various barriers often hinder our ability to fully engage with our communities. These barriers can be social, cultural, economic, or even self-imposed. Overcoming these obstacles

requires an understanding of their root causes and a commitment to dismantling them.

One significant barrier to community engagement is a lack of awareness and understanding. People may not be aware of the diverse opportunities and resources available within their own communities. Educating ourselves about local events, initiatives, and organizations enables us to actively participate and contribute to the betterment of our community.

Another barrier is the fear of judgment and rejection. Many individuals hesitate to engage with their community due to concerns about how they will be perceived or accepted. Overcoming this fear requires cultivating self-confidence and recognizing that everyone has something valuable to offer. By embracing our unique qualities and perspectives, we can contribute to our community in ways that are meaningful and beneficial to those around us.

Fostering a Supportive Community:
Building a supportive and connected community is a shared responsibility. It requires a proactive approach from individuals, as well as the efforts of community leaders, organizations, and institutions. When everyone comes together with a common goal of fostering positive relationships, the potential for growth and transformation becomes limitless.

Creating inclusive spaces that promote diversity and equal participation is paramount. By acknowledging and celebrating the unique characteristics and contributions of all individuals, we can foster an environment where everyone feels valued and respected. Furthermore, encouraging collaboration and mutual support is essential in nurturing a strong community. When individuals and organizations work together, they can share resources, knowledge, and experiences, amplifying the impact of their efforts. Collaboration also fosters a sense of belonging and reminds us that we are not alone in our endeavors.

The Ripple Effect of Positive Relationships:

Building positive relationships and engaging with our community not only has immediate benefits for our own well-being but also creates a ripple effect that extends far beyond our personal connections. When we lead by example and foster an environment of respect, compassion, and unity, others are inspired to do the same. This creates a continuous cycle of positivity, where each positive interaction builds upon the one before it.

Moreover, by actively engaging with our community, we become catalysts for change. Through collective action and shared values, we can address societal issues, promote social justice, and create a more equitable world for all.

Connection and community engagement are pivotal for personal growth, societal harmony, and the overall well-being of individuals and communities alike. By embracing the power and importance of building positive relationships, we create an environment where everyone can thrive. Let us cultivate empathy, actively engage with our communities, and embrace the endless possibilities that come with genuine human connections. Together, we can build a collectively empowered and prosperous future.